W9-CZR-996

A MOST SUPERIOR LAND

LIFE IN THE UPPER PENINSULA OF MICHIGAN

TwoPeninsula Press
Copyright 1983
Second Printing, March 1987

PUBLISHER: Russell McKee
COMPILER: David M. Frimodig
EDITOR: Susan Newhof Pyle
BOOK DESIGN: Glenna Segall
GRAPHICS ASSISTANT: Leianne Wright
COLOR SEPARATIONS: Image Arts, Lansing
PRINTING: The John Henry Company, Lansing
BINDING: John H. Dekker & Sons, Grand Rapids
PAPER: 70-pound Black and White Gloss by the
    Mead Corporation, Escanaba
TYPE: Text in 11/13 English Times, set on the
    EditWriter 7500.

Library of Congress Catalog Number: 83-620003
ISBN Number: 0-941912-03-5

Copyright © 1983 by Michigan Natural Resources
Magazine, Department of Natural Resources, State
of Michigan, James J. Blanchard, Governor. All
rights of this book are reserved, and may not be
reprinted or otherwise reproduced without the
expressed written permission of the publisher.

*A Most Superior Land, Life In The Upper
Peninsula of Michigan* is Volume IV of the
Michigan Heritage Series, and is a publication of
TwoPeninsula Press, a unit of

NATURAL RESOURCES MAGAZINE
Box 30034, Lansing, MI 48909

photo courtesy of Superior View, Marquette

A Note About This Book

The book you hold is the fourth in our growing series of Michigan Heritage volumes, books that herald the beauties and lively interests of our state. Some have suggested we keep Michigan a secret, worried that there may not be enough for everyone, but we can cope with outsiders here, never fear.

Coping, in fact, is a way of life in the U.P., and one of its many subterranean charms. Those who pass through the peninsula too quickly see only long green vistas, little towns, some nice scenery. Those who tarry see a bit more—the awareness and honesty of people who live close to the land, the quick wit that's a hallmark of the peninsula, the independent spirit that keeps bankers and janitors and mechanics and mayors all equal in community stature. Those who finally get so tangled up listening to all the talk and humor and dialects simply give up and move there. But as noted above, Upper Peninsula residents can cope with the quick, the tarry, and the new natives with equal ease.

So many have contributed to this project that we are humbled by the energy it contains. Lay it down carefully, it may explode. But, as always, a few led the way. David Mac Frimodig of Laurium was the generator, planner, organizer, and general foreman. Susan Newhof Pyle of the magazine staff picked up in Lansing where Frimodig, in far-off Laurium, had to leave off. It's her first big edit and a thoroughly excellent effort. Glenna Segall and Leianne Wright of the magazine's graphic staff organized the photos and graphics out of literally thousands of possibilities. Jack Deo of Marquette generously opened his growing and remarkable collection of old photos for use in the book. As for the authors, please meet them on pages 184-85.

This book was published by the TwoPeninsula Press, a unit of the Michigan Natural Resources Magazine program, an "Enterprise Fund" agency in the Michigan Department of Natural Resources. The Michigan Legislature has authorized us to publish the magazine, books, and related materials, but we receive no tax money for any aspect of this work. The total program, including salaries, printing, paper, overhead—everything—operates solely on voluntary magazine subscriptions and book sales revenues. It's a bootstrap operation extolling Michigan values that costs taxpayers nothing. We hope you enjoy it as much as we've enjoyed putting it together.

Russell McKee
July 1983

LAKE SUPERIOR

AND THE NORTHERN PART OF

MICHIGAN

1855

Fort William

Kaministiquia R.

Mt Kays Mt
1000 ft

Thunder Cape

Pie Island

Sturgeon Bay

Princes Bay

Spur I.

Thompsons I.

Mt Murray
Cove

Victoria I.

Todds Pt.

Goose L.

Pigeon R.

Pigeon Bay

Grand Portage

Washington Har.

ISLE ROYALE

Pt. Porphyry

Gull Islet

Passage I.

Battrea

Boonda

MINNESOTA

Boat Har.

LAKE

SU

Eagle Har.

Copper Har.

Eagle R.

Agate Har.

North West

Two Islands R.

Baptism R.

Cliff Mine

Eagle Riv.

Portage

Salmon Trout R.

Traverse I.

Gooseberry R.

APOSTLE ISLANDS

Bartletts I.

Stocktons I.

Mana R.

Keweenaw Bay

Tobacco

Knife R.

FOND DU LAC

POINT DE TOUR

Madeline I.

Lone Rock

Porcupine

Franklin

Ontonagon R.

Ontonagon

Fire R.

L'Anse

Huron

St. Louis R.

Superior

Rasbery Cr.

La Pointe

Chaqwamegon Pt.

Gray R.

Iron R.

Minnesota Mine

Chaqwamegon Bay

Fish Cr.

Maskeg R.

Montreal I.

ONTONAGON

Black R.

MARQUE

Mach

Ayanike Lakes

Burnt Wood R.

Kagino L.

Meminis L.

Namebn L.

Weyekwa L.

Pine Wood L.

Vieux Desert L.

Menominee R.

Sandy L.

Brule

Machigaaig

Kinonje L.

Shishib L.

Ajasowi L.

Mandowish Lo.

Trout L.

Brule or Wesacota R.

Manitosawin L.

W

Waswagoning L.

Perch L.

Twin F.

L. Arb

Kawawye L.

L. Courte Oreille

Chippewa M.

Michicoril L.

Oshtigwan L.

Lac du Port

Muskas R.

Gt Bekuenesec Falls

Lit. Bekuenesec

Buffalo R.

Lac Flambeau dore

White Fish L.

Zarto Wissopo R.

CON

S

Squirrel R.

Chippewa

Maridowish R.

South Fork

Yellow R.

Whaypaw R.

Rapids

Stanisswing R.

Wolf River

Fishtago R.

IN

Portage

Black R.

Wisconsin R.

Rapids

Pine R.

Orano R.

photo courtesy of Michigan State Archives

Table Of Contents

photo courtesy of Michigan State Archives

Holding The U.P. Still

The Upper Peninsula of Michigan has been a favorite subject for photographers since 1850. Early references to their work appeared in the *Lake Superior Journal* in 1850 and 1851 when C.L. Weed of Sault Ste. Marie, and R. Cormely of Eagle River offered daguerreotypes, one of the earliest forms of photography. Mining towns and lumber camps were brimming with people eager to have a "likeness" made by this fledgling art form. It was the shiny, silver-coated daguerreotypes that first captured the construction of the Soo Locks in 1855, the locks being the gate that opened the U.P. to greater economic activity and more photographers.

By the 1860s, the wet-plate negative had replaced the daguerreotype, giving photographers the opportunity to photograph U.P. lumberjacks, miners, and sailors outdoors in their working environments with a backdrop of the peninsula's beautiful landscapes. But photographing outside the shelter of the studio was not an easy task. Fragile glass negatives had to be coated with light-sensitive chemicals, exposed while the plates were still wet, and developed immediately. The process required a dark tent which was carried along with the heavy, bulky camera equipment often weighing as much as a hundred pounds.

By the 1880s, nearly every town in the U.P. had a practicing photographer. Many had been artists who adopted the camera as an extension of their profession. Some called their studios "Art Galleries" and made them as elegant as surrounding Detroit, Chicago and Milwaukee establishments. But just as often, a tent or a rough-hewn log cabin served as the photographer's place of business. It also became common for U.P. photographers to operate several branch studios throughout the peninsula, whose openings often coincided with the sinking of a new mine shaft.

By the turn of the century, more than one hundred professional photographers were working throughout the U.P., and many are well remembered for their efforts in documenting life styles of the people of the peninsula. In Sault Ste. Marie, A.E. Young and W.J. Bell captured many views of the shipping industry, as well as life among the Chippewa Indians and fishing in the St. Mary's Rapids. Some photographers used special techniques, such as Adolph Isler's "Birds-eye Views" which he obtained by scaling the towering smokestacks of the copper smelters. J.W. Nara will be best remembered for his extensive coverage of the 1913 copper strikes and the tragic Italian Hall Disaster of Calumet.

Theodore Hall was a young Upper Peninsula photographer from the Negaunee area. He is shown here in the quiet waters of a channel at Isle Royale during the late 1800s.

9

Eskil's Art Gallery,

215 HUGHITT STREET.

IRON MOUNTAIN, = = MICHIGAN.

Duplicates of this picture can be had at any time.

photo courtesy of Superior View, Marquette

10

A. LIDBERG'S
ART GALLERY,

ISHPEMING, MICH.

photo courtesy of Superior View, Marquette

In Marquette County alone, more than 40 shutterbugs operated before 1900. Best known was Brainard F. Childs whose studio, Child's Art Gallery, operated for almost ninety years. Childs was originally a painter from Vermont. He went to work for photographer C.B. Brubaker in the 1860s, and before long, was producing photos of stunning beauty and composition. While he first became known for his skilled portraits, some of his greatest achievements were in stereo photographs which produce a 3-dimensional image.

In the early 1870s Childs took an Indian guide and sailed a small Mackinaw boat entirely around Lake Superior. This brave excursion resulted in more than four hundred exquisite stereo views of the Lake Superior shoreline and the area's inhabitants. He printed and marketed these views as ''Gems of Lake Superior,'' and they gave the country its first look at life around the big lake.

George Shiras III spent much of his life in Marquette and took top honors at the Paris World's Fair in 1900. He and Charles Cole, of Ishpeming, took first and second respectively at the 1904 St. Louis World's Fair. Both men were pioneers in flashlight photography. Cole worked a mile beneath the earth's surface to capture the world of miners, while Shiras set cameras with tripwires to produce the first photos of wildlife in their natural habitat. He became *National Geographic's* first wildlife photographer and wrote a two volume work entitled *Hunting Wildlife with Camera and Flashlight*.

Many other great photographers have dotted the peninsula in the past century, leaving a visual legacy of life in Michigan's north country. The fruits of their labor now adorn the walls of museums and historical societies across the state, and are tucked away in private albums and dusty attics. This book has gathered some of the all-time favorite photographs, along with many which have never-before been published. And if it's true that a picture is worth a thousand words, you have a lot of exciting reading to do!

photo courtesy of Superior View, Marquette

These elegant studio advertisements were printed on the backs of portrait photographs.

11

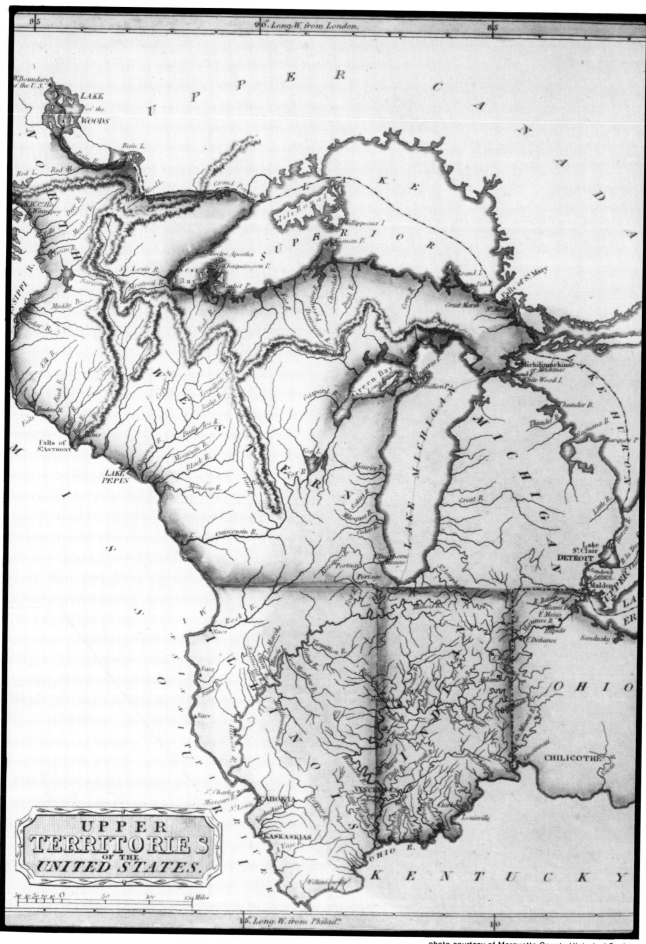

photo courtesy of Marquette County Historical Society

12

This Jeweled Peninsula

It's a jagged finger of land, this Upper Peninsula of Michigan, sharing as it does a common border with Wisconsin, then running its ragged coastline eastward 350 miles to meet Canada at the St. Mary's River. On the southern border, the "other peninsula" of Michigan lies beyond the Straits of Mackinac. Some have thought the U.P. should be its own state—Superior. Some say it was merely a part of Ohio the Ohioans didn't want—an obvious reference to the Toledo War, a border dispute between Ohio and Michigan in 1835 over who owned Toledo. Ohio got Toledo and Michigan got the Upper Peninsula as a consolation prize. Consolation indeed! Nestled between Lake Superior to the north and Lakes Huron and Michigan to the south, this jeweled land remained largely an enigma to the outside world until 1840. That year, Dr. Douglass Houghton published his famous mineral report of the region, and the boom which ensued rivaled the California gold rush for drama and intensity. Thousands of eager pioneers streamed north and west from all over the eastern half of the nation. Houghton's careful account of mineral wealth was twisted, expanded, blown out of proportion and republished throughout the nation. Deck space was at a premium on all boats that traveled up Lakes Michigan and Huron to Superior. There were no overland roads, but hopefuls hacked their way through the wilderness and followed rivers to reach that well-coppered land.

Needless to say, for most, the bubble soon burst. Clusters of log buildings that sprang up overnight around mine shafts occasionally became towns, some of which still exist today. But most died an early death beside the empty holes and dashed hopes of their builders. Those miners who struck paying veins, however, remained to alter the face of this rugged land, and by the end of the Civil War, the onrush of mining and logging and settlement had put an end to the historic isolation of the peninsula.

Poignant reminders of this history may still be seen in their natural, if dilapidated, state on the old copper ranges of the peninsula. Copper was indeed successfully mined for many decades on a narrow belt of hilly land all the way from Ontonagon to Eagle River near the tip of the Keweenaw Peninsula. There are dozens of old mining structures left here, as though asleep and awaiting the return of long removed populations. A ghost-like atmosphere surrounds the rusting old head frames and shaft houses, shafts that in some places lead down 10,000 feet or deeper to veins that still contain

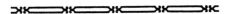

The map at left was published in 1824, 16 years before survey crews had completed their work in the Lower Peninsula and moved into the eastern third of the Upper Peninsula. Very little was known about the vast wilderness region until Dr. Douglass Houghton published his famous mineral report of the region in 1840.

substantial quantities of the purest copper the world has ever seen—then or now.

Not all of it was deep in the ground, however. The old Cliff Mine—earliest in the region—paid a dividend of $60,000 to stockholders in 1849, five years after digging began, and much of that pure copper came in the first several hundred feet below the surface. But imagine climbing 800 feet of ladder to get home from work each day! The Minesota Mine (that's how it was spelled) was another productive hole near present Ontonagon, and became famous for its huge masses of pure copper. In 1856, a 46-foot-long, 400-plus ton mass of copper was discovered in this mine. Many such huge masses had to be bypassed, and a few are still underground today, simply because there has been no cost effective way to cut them up and get them out. Geologists believe that as the price of copper escalates, some of these mines will eventually be reopened and the remaining large masses will be recovered.

Iron mining gave birth to the port city of Marquette. A harbor of refuge, the town became the natural outlet for the ores that began pouring forth from the iron hills of Negaunee and Ishpeming. First shipments of ore were hauled over a crude plank road in wagons drawn by mules, but the huge volume of ore to be transported brought about construction of the Iron Mountain Railroad in 1857, connecting the port of Marquette with the iron mines a short way to the west. In those days, all labor was done by hand and sledgehammer. Holes were drilled in solid rock, packed with black powder, and the whole lot was detonated at the end of each day. On the following day, the loosened ore was hammered down to size, loaded shovel by shovel onto mule carts, and hauled to the docks in Marquette. One trip took most of the day. After reaching the port, the ore was laboriously shoveled by hand onto the dock, then reloaded into wheelbarrows and wheeled into the holds of waiting vessels. It took from three to six days and lots of blisters to load a standard 200 to 300 ton vessel, quite a contrast to modern operations!

Another problem encountered mutually by the iron and copper mining concerns was the transportation bottleneck at Sault Ste. Marie. All southbound traffic flowed out of Lake Superior into the St. Mary's River, so all vessels were halted at the river's turbulent rapids. There, the vessels had to be unloaded, the ore was hauled down below the rapids, and then reloaded into other ships that carried it south to smelters at Chicago, Detroit, Cleveland, and other ports. This went on for about ten years before Congress authorized a right-of-way for the canal and gave Michigan 750,000 acres of federal land to use as payment for construction of the lock project. On June 18, 1855, the work was complete and the steamer *Illinois* became the first vessel to pass through the 350-foot-long State Lock with a load of ore.

The canal was one of two leading influences that opened the U.P. to major development—the other being the Civil War. During the first year of operation, for example, about 14,000 tons of freight passed through the locks. Ten years later, during the Civil War, this had increased to 284,000 tons, most of it copper, iron ore, and grain. The war had opened with the peninsula still holding only three percent of the state's population. During the winter, the tiny,

photo courtesy of Chippewa County Historical Society

photo courtesy of Superior View, Marquette

photo courtesy of Superior View, Marquette

Pictured in the top photograph is an Indian fisherman with his nets. The Chippewa migrated to the rapids area of the St. Mary's River during the 16th Century and found the waters filled with fine whitefish. They established a thriving village which was largely sustained by the river. The Indians at center were photographed while fishing the St. Mary's in 1892. While the early lock projects brought prosperity to many regions of the Upper Peninsula and aided the North during the Civil War, they reduced the river's useage as a fishing grounds. The dog sled team in the bottom photo was on a Lake Superior mail run when it was captured on film in the 1870s.

15

photo by Bell, courtesy of Chippewa County Historical Society

photo by J.W. Nara, courtesy of Superior View, Marquette

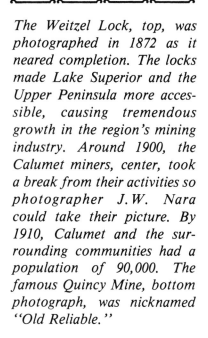

The Weitzel Lock, top, was photographed in 1872 as it neared completion. The locks made Lake Superior and the Upper Peninsula more accessible, causing tremendous growth in the region's mining industry. Around 1900, the Calumet miners, center, took a break from their activities so photographer J.W. Nara could take their picture. By 1910, Calumet and the surrounding communities had a population of 90,000. The famous Quincy Mine, bottom photograph, was nicknamed "Old Reliable."

photo courtesy of Marquette County Historical Society

16

remote communities of the region were cut off from the rest of the world. There were no telegraph connections until after the war, and the only mail delivery was by occasional dog sled from Green Bay. All shipping stopped at all ports when the Soo Locks plugged with ice. But the demand for iron and copper during the war brought Houghton County copper mines into their own, surpassing the earlier Keweenaw and Ontonagon mines by a wide margin. The picture in the iron hills was just as rosy. A mining report issued in 1873 noted that three companies had been operating on the Marquette range in 1854, while 40 operated there 19 years later. From 3000 tons of ore shipped in 1854, the total rose to nearly 1,200,000 tons in 1873. Several larger locks were later built to accommodate the increasing number and size of freighters.

In the post-Civil War period, cities that had earlier been mining boom towns began to grow again. Important communities such as Ontonagon, Houghton-Hancock, the iron ports of Marquette and Escanaba, and the lumber town of Menominee began to emerge. By 1910, Calumet and the surrounding communities had a total of 90,000 people. This general growth also pushed development of the U.P.'s other great resource—timber. Before 1870, there had been minimal use of these great forests. But the pace of logging stepped up as the tide of immigration, mining, and land development grew. Lumber from the lake states was used to build Chicago and other Midwest metropolitan areas, as well as farm settlements on the prairies and the railroads that connected those two regions. It was thought that the seemingly endless Upper Peninsula forests would last forever, but most large trees were cut within a 15-year period. In 1888, the average log provided about 200 board feet of lumber; by 1916, it had dropped to one-sixth that amount. Shipment figures in the last two decades of the 19th Century were staggering. The Menominee River Boom Company eventually controlled all traffic on that important river, and during the peak year of 1889, this one company shipped 642 million feet of prime timber.

Although most of the great timber stands were cut by the 1930s, lumbering is once again a thriving industry in the Upper Peninsula. Because of sophisticated forest management practices, and diligent reforestation—some of which began 50 years ago with the Civilian Conservation Corps—the peninsula's timber resources are getting better and local lumber-oriented businesses are growing. The face of farming has changed, but it still makes important contributions to the peninsula's economy. New methods of reclamation have kept iron mining an active industry, and tourism, which grew steadily after 1900, now brings economic relief year-round. Upper Peninsula visitors have a collage of magnificent settings before them—from Mackinac, Les Cheneaux, and island groups in the St. Mary's River, to the sparkling sand and gravel beaches and cliff-lined shores found on three adjacent Great Lakes, to the ghost towns and forgotten mining works on the jagged Keweenaw Peninsula. A rich and colorful heritage manifests itself and will continue to draw visitors searching for a verdant vacationland. Perhaps John St. John said it best in an 1846 publication: "Gentlemen, you can find life itself in the Lake Superior region provided you can be pleased with waterfalls, lakes, and mountains. The air is bracing yet soft and natives all live to a great age."

photo by Childs Art Gallery, courtesy of Superior View, Marquette

So Many Different People

We are, as the late President John F. Kennedy so aptly put it, a nation of immigrants. And perhaps in no section of our nation has this fact been more evident than in the Upper Peninsula. People from almost every nation in northern, western, central and southern Europe, the British Isles, and Scandinavia have made important contributions to the growth and development of this area.

The first major immigrant group to have a significant impact on the region's growth and development was the Cornish. There were many earlier peoples—the Algonquin Indian groups, French traders and trappers, the English colonists and military figures. But these groups were always small in number and much more nomadic, and their impact on the land was less when compared to that of the Cornish who arrived first in the 1850s.

Cornwall, that slender tip of land forming southwestern England, contained some of the world's richest copper mines. In the first three decades of the 19th Century, those mines produced two-thirds of the world's copper. But by the 1850s, that industry was dying, a victim of competition from American mines then being developed. Cornish miners began leaving their homeland, and by the late 1850s many had found their way to Michigan's Copper Country. Once here, they began to revolutionize mining methods. They introduced drilling by hand with sledges, blasting with black gunpowder, and hauling with a Cornish "kibble," a small handcar powered by a Cornish "horse whim." Steam-powered stamps for removing metal from the surrounding stone quickly came into use. Their wooden "hammer handles" supported two-hundred-pound iron heads that could drop on the rock twenty times per minute.

During the 1850s and 1860s the Copper Country experienced flush times and towns began sprouting the typical frontier institutions—from rough-and-tumble saloons to what passed for miners' boarding houses. These outposts were made up predominantly of single Cornish and Irish laborers, men whose lives consisted mainly of working in the mines, eating bad food, drinking worse whiskey, and gaining their social contacts through fist fights. Realizing the need for a more stable labor supply, the mine owners began to furnish housing for their miners, and soon the number of miners with families began to grow. Churches and schools began to appear, and with these came the beginning of real communities.

From 1872 until the early 1880s economic conditions in the copper mines remained rather stable. Work was plentiful, and the

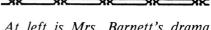

At left is Mrs. Barnett's drama group from Ishpeming, photographed by B.F. Childs around 1890. Seeking companionship in their new surroundings, immigrants often organized musical groups, charities, athletic clubs, and other associations shortly after they arrived here.

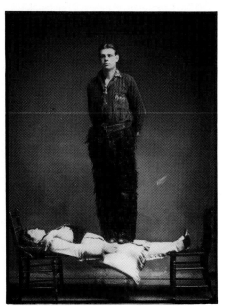

photo by G.A. Werner, courtesy of Superior View, Marquette

photo by Miller, courtesy of Superior View, Marquette

The magician and strong-lady team, above, had this picture taken in Ishpeming about 1900. Notice that the supporting chair has been painted out! Above right, these two women from the Miller family of Negaunee posed for this photograph about 1900.

area's Cornish, Irish, French-speaking Canadien, and German residents learned to live and work in harmony. By 1870, there were also 14,000 miners and lumberjacks working in the peninsula's three iron districts. Two-thirds of the workers were Cornish or Irish.

In the years following the Civil War, several thousand Finnish, Swedish, and Norwegian immigrants settled in the Upper Peninsula, most coming directly from their homelands, rather than from older Scandinavian settlements in the U.S. The Norwegians and the Swedes came because their homelands could no longer provide enough suitable farmland to support their growing populations. They also came because of encouraging letters from Scandinavian pioneers, favorable reports from returned immigrants, guidebooks, and poor harvests and hard times at home. Many Swedes came to work as "contract laborers." The mine company paid their transportation to Michigan, and the immigrants agreed to work for the company until their wages equaled the cost of their transportation. Once these terms were filled, the immigrants were free to leave the company, but most stayed on.

Beginning in 1863, Finland experienced a form of social and cultural awakening. The country was changing from a rural to an industrial nation, and thousands began to leave their homes for life elsewhere. Large numbers of these people came to settle in America. As with the Swedes and Norwegians, some Finns came to Michigan because they'd heard about the northern farmland and forests. Others were contacted in the homeland by agents representing various railroad and mining companies. From 1864 to 1884, agents convinced some eight hundred Finnish miners that the good life awaited them in Michigan's mines. These miners wrote and urged others to come, and by 1911, one-quarter of the workers on the Gogebic Iron Range were Finns, most of whom had arrived without any effort on the part of their employers.

Scandinavians who compared conditions in their homeland to those in the U.P. felt that the chance to begin earning a living immediately after arriving was sufficient reason to come here. Some immigrants, especially the Finns, hoped that the economic opportunities here might make it possible to accumulate sufficient savings to purchase a farm. Along with a willingness to work, Scandinavian

photo by G.A. Werner, courtesy of Superior View, Marquette

photo by G.A. Werner, courtesy of Superior View, Marquette

settlers had a high literacy rate, very little liquid capital (one historian has given us an estimate of fifty dollars per family,) a conservative religious outlook, the dream of finding great wealth, an associative spirit, and the physical strength to match conditions.

Michigan's Finns, more than any other group, have written about their immigrant experience here and, even more importantly, have been collecting source material about this experience. Most of it is housed in the Finnish-American Historical Library at Suomi College, Hancock, founded by Michigan Finns, and the only Finnish institution of higher learning in the U.S. From these materials, or from books and articles based on them, we gain a deep appreciation for these hardy pioneers. Seeking companionship shortly after they arrived in Michigan, the Finns rapidly organized associations such as charities, religious congregations, temperance societies, musical groups, and athletic clubs. From the iron and copper mines in the 1880s to agricultural, educational, and business pursuits in the Twentieth Century, the Finns have retained a sense of community life through their activities and shared experiences.

English-speaking Canadians and French-speaking Canadiens began to come to the Upper Pensinsula in fairly substantial numbers in the two decades before the Civil War. In most cases they were drawn to the region by the twin lures of location and strong possibilities for employment. Unfortunately for historians, however, the Canadians were rapidly assimilated into American society and, as a result, left few written records dealing with their immigrant experiences. The French-speaking Canadiens, on the other hand, have provided a fairly rich record of their achievements which tend to document the fact that, by the late Nineteenth Century, there were significant Canadien communities in Marquette, Houghton, and Menominee Counties. Most Canadiens in these and other Upper Peninsula areas were employed in the mines, while others entered agriculture, fishing, or domestic service. Like many of their fellow immigrants, the Canadiens were interested in preserving their cultural identity. The most active among them formed national societies, published French newspapers, and worked for the organization of Roman Catholic parishes served by Canadien priests. That they failed to create a lasting sense of community

What secret organization or fraternity could the men, above, have belonged to? We have never been able to identify them, and know only that the photo was taken by G.A. Werner about 1900. Above left, Werner took this photo of the Ishpeming Finnish Band at about the same time. The blur in the front row is a small child who moved during the long exposure time that was needed to make this picture.

among the state's French-speaking residents was due much more to the scattered settlement pattern of Canadien emigration to Michigan than to any lack of zeal on the part of the movement's leaders. There was little group organization or solidarity among these French-speaking people, particularly when the French experience in this area is compared to that of other nationalities.

The Germans and the Irish also played an important role in the settlement of the U.P. By the 1840s, the German immigrant became, in the minds of a number of Michigan legislators, the ideal settler. Germans were seen as industrious, religious, educated, and often interested in establishing educational institutions. For almost fifty years, political leaders in our state made certain that Michigan immigrant guidebooks were published in German, as well as English, and that both versions were sent to Germany. Although such efforts were quite successful in convincing Germans that they should come to Michigan, the vast majority became farmers in the southern part of the state. One well-planned effort to bring Germans north of the Straits to work for the Munising Iron Company in 1872 was a complete failure. The "advance guard" of the projected *Colonie Saxonia* reported unfavorably on Upper Peninsula weather. By 1900, however, there were Germans living and working in all of the peninsula's counties.

The Irish possessed all the tools for economic success in the Upper Peninsula during its boom period of development. Like the Cornish, the Finns, and the Canadians, the Irish also came to the Midwest with the hope of finding employment. They had been driven from Ireland by repressive land laws and a series of devastating potato famines, and most arrived here flat broke. They worked whatever jobs they could find, and from sledgehammer to hoe, no job was too difficult. Once they found that work in a certain area was generally available, the call went out to the homeland. The result was a steady stream of hardworking laborers arriving in the Upper Peninsula when unskilled labor was an absolute necessity.

From the late 19th Century until the immigration quota system was established in the 1920s, the country of origin of most of our immigrants gradually changed from the nations of

The group of nurses, below, posed at G.A. Werner's studio about 1900. Below right, these young Norwegian women with their stylish tucks and bows posed for B.F. Childs about 1890.

photo by G.A. Werner, courtesy of Superior View

photo by Childs Art Gallery, courtesy of Superior View

western Europe, Scandinavia, and the British Isles to the countries of eastern and southern Europe. Usually described as the "new" immigration, this population movement brought thousands of Poles, Hungarians, Italians, Croatians, and Yugoslavs to Michigan. Although they differed culturally from the "old" immigrants and came in greater numbers, the new immigrants were remarkably similar to the old in their reasons for migrating, in the skills they possessed, and in their willingness to adjust to new surroundings.

Beyond the world of work, the "new" immigrants gathered in separate ethnic neighborhoods and began to build churches, organize fraternal and social clubs, and publish newspapers in their native language. Such "ingathering" was important to the newcomers, but it aroused the antagonism and suspicion of the "old" immigrants, most of whom had by now been largely assimilated into the mainstream of American life.

Two major events changed the Upper Peninsula's immigration pattern from the course it had followed for more than 50 years. In 1913-14, crippling labor strikes almost halted copper mining, and thousands of residents left the peninsula for jobs in urban centers, particularly Detroit, where established ethnic neighborhoods and the developing auto industry beckoned. This was especially true of the Italians, Poles and Yugoslavs. In the mid-1920s, Congress established the first immigration quotas for each country, a move that slowed all U.S. immigration to a trickle. With these two changes occurring in a period of about ten years, the old open-to-all chapter in the peninsula's immigration history ended.

Those who have remained in the Upper Peninsula are reminded daily of the area's rich heritage. For a few groups, most notably the Finns, the region is still a center of important ethnic activity. In recent years a growing number of younger people, some of them descendants of the peninsula's Nineteenth Century immigrants, have either returned to the north country or have elected to stay and become part of the region's future. It may well be that their back-to-the-land movement will spark a new flow of immigrants to this magnificent region, and in so doing begin a new chapter in the area's unique social history.

The two men pictured below are members of the Ancient Order of Foresters, photographed in Ishpeming at the B.F. Childs Art Gallery about 1900. Below left, this horse-drawn delivery wagon was from the Cooperativa Italiana in the Iron Mountain area.

photo courtesy of Menominee Range Museum, Iron Mountain

photo by Childs Art Gallery, courtesy of Superior View

23

photo courtesy of Michigan Technological University Archives

24

Superior Copper And Iron

On a chilly March day in 1848, Samuel O. Knapp and J.B. Townsend were following fresh porcupine tracks in hopes of a meal, when they discovered a small opening to an ancient cave. With pick and shovel they opened the hole, searched through the debris, and found numerous stone hammers and mauls and other evidence of prehistoric human work. Further digging turned up great chunks of native copper which had been too large for the early miners to cut up and move, along with a well-defined vein of native copper in the bedrock. We know, now, that the Keweenaw Peninsula and Isle Royale had hundreds of these ancient diggings, some more than 4,000 years old. The prehistoric miners had recovered the "float" copper that was on the beaches and in the stream beds, and the copper in the bedrock itself. They built fires against the rock to get it hot and then threw water on it, causing it to spall, or break up. The copper ores, for the most part, were native or elemental copper, with some native silver.

Because the early European explorers and missionaries had not learned of the prehistoric miners from the Indians they met, it was assumed that those earlier people were of a non-Indian race. More recent studies suggest that local Indians *were* descendants of these ancient miners, but that their legends had not survived, perhaps because their beliefs and superstitions tended to have them avoid any references to the copper or to the iron.

In 1765, Captain Jonathan Carver wrote of his discovery of "mines of virgin copper" and mentioned the Ontonagon River. In 1771, a group of miners came over from Great Britain, led by Alexander Henry, but they were not successful in recovering any copper. Fortunately for what was about to happen, the federal government decided in 1795 to survey and subdivide all the lands west of the existing states. By 1840, the survey reached the north extremity of the Lower Peninsula, and in May, 1840, deputy surveyor W.A. Burt carried the survey into the Upper Peninsula. For about two hundred years, the standard surveyor's tool had sighting arms rotating around a compass. In 1833, Burt had encountered some local magnetic attraction in Wisconsin that interfered with his surveying. As a solution to the problem, he invented a solar compass in 1835 which he used five years later while working in the Upper Peninsula.

General Lewis Cass organized an expedition in 1820 to explore the south shore of Lake Superior and on into Minnesota. One member of the party was Henry R. Schoolcraft who acted as geologist

The copper miners at left are about to descend to their work areas, 10,000 feet below ground.

25

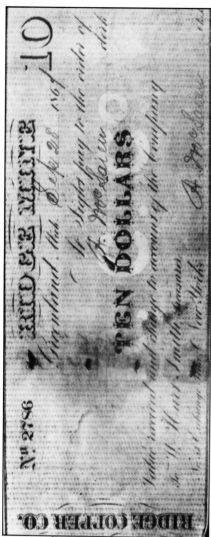

photo courtesy of Cleveland-Cliffs

Remote mining towns were often cut off from the larger cities during winter months, preventing delivery of mail, supplies, and even money. Many of the mining companies turned to printing their own currency, which was widely accepted. It was referred to as copper money or iron money. Pictured above is copper money, issued by the Ridge Copper Company on September 28, 1864. The copper ingots, above right, are stacked on the dock at Houghton-Hancock, awaiting shipment.

photo courtesy of DNR

and mineralogist. He described finding "virgin copper" near Portage Entry, and he saw the "Ontonagon Boulder." In 1826, General Cass negotiated a treaty at Fond du Lac providing for the surrender of Indian mineral rights in the lands affected. Schoolcraft returned in 1832 with a party that included Dr. Douglass Houghton, medical doctor and naturalist as well as mayor of Detroit. Under the direction of Michigan's first governor, Stevens T. Mason, Houghton became the first State Geologist. His initial project was to spend the summer and fall of 1840 in the Upper Peninsula, and a portion of his report of February 1, 1841 said: "While I am fully satisfied that the mineral district of our state will prove a source of eventual and steady increasing wealth to our people, I cannot fail to have before me the fear that it may prove the ruin of hundreds of adventurers who will visit it with expectations never to be realized."

Houghton's fears were well-founded. His reports stimulated the Michigan "Copper Boom" in 1843, five years before the California Gold Rush. A federal office was established at Copper Harbor in 1843 to issue mineral leases. By 1845, that office had 327 leases on record, held by a swarm of prospectors who had come to the Copper Country braving the rigors of insects by summer and heavy snows by winter. Many were poorly prepared for the hardships, and losses to exposure, sickness, and suicide were heavy.

The copper boom covered the Keweenaw Peninsula and extended westerly. The Indians called the Peninsula *"Ke-wai-wo-na,"* translated as "the place we go around." Three principal areas of search emerged—the Eagle River area, the Houghton-Portage Lake area, and the western area near Ontonagon. The discovery of the Calumet area came a little later. Many prospectors labored hard and long only to fulfill Houghton's prediction of failure. There were also, however, many interesting success stories.

A Pittsburgh pharmacist named John Hays caught the copper fever and came to Copper Harbor in July, 1843, with the advice and financial support of his physician, Dr. C.G. Hussey. He met with a prospector named Jim Raymond from Boston, who had the distinction of having registered the first three claims at the Copper Harbor mineral lease office. Hays secured an option for a one-sixth interest,

photo by Butler, courtesy of Cleveland-Cliffs

and returned to Pittsburgh with an enthusiastic report. Dr. Hussey and several other investors agreed to continue financing the venture which eventually produced the Pittsburgh and Boston Mining Company, and the Cliff Mine just south of Eagle River. By 1849, the Cliff Mine paid its first dividend and was the first mine in the Copper Country to do so. In fact, it continued to pay its owners handsomely and was a bonanza until it was sold in 1871, having paid dividends totalling $2,280,000.

The pit belonging to the ancient miners, onto which Knapp and Townsend had stumbled, contained a piece of mass copper raised more than five feet above the floor, resting on cribbing. That was as high as the ancients had been able to elevate it. Knapp directed that a shaft be sunk at that location, and it hit solid copper. From that discovery came the successful Minesota (spelled with one "n") Mine which paid its first dividend in 1852, and subsequently became famous for the size of its mass copper. In 1856 the miners hit the "granddaddy" of them all, a piece of copper at least 46 feet long by 18 feet at its widest and 8.5 feet at its thickest. It was estimated to weigh more than 500 tons. What a task it was to cut up the mass copper, as the miners' only tools were chisels, sledgehammers and black gunpowder! The mine paid $1,750,000 in dividends on a capital investment of $436,000, and produced more than 35 million pounds of copper.

On November 17, 1846, owners of the Portage Mining Company and the Northwestern Mining Company met in Marshall, Michigan to settle a dispute as to who owned the lands on the hill above Hancock. Instead of arguing, they decided to form the Quincy Mining Company to work the site. The mine opened in 1856, and paid its first dividend on July 31, 1862. Thomas F. Mason presided over Quincy from 1858 to 1899, and under his regime, the company prospered and grew. He provided a boarding house and family homes for the miners, as well as a hospital funded by compulsory payments of fifty cents a month for single employees and a dollar a month for married men and their families. The company also built a large hotel, gave land for churches in Hancock, built the school and rented it to the school district. Quincy paid dividends for many

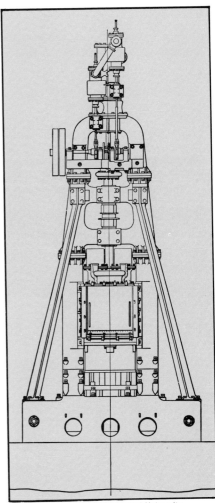

courtesy of Michigan Technological University Archives and Copper Country Historical Collections

Above is a drawing of a steam powered stamp mill from 1905. Note how clean the "Man Hoist" engine and working area, above left, were kept. This photo was taken about 1880.

photo courtesy of Copper Range Railroad

photo courtesy of Cleveland-Cliffs

photo by Homburg, courtesy of Cleveland-Cliffs

years, and mining continued there until September 1, 1945, earning it the nickname "Old Reliable."

The giant of the copper mining companies was the Calumet and Hecla Consolidated Copper Company, known to everyone as the C & H. A colorful tale is told about the discovery of this incredibly rich lode. Billy Royal, the proprietor of a roadhouse located about midway between Portage Lake and Eagle River, asked a young surveyor and civil engineer named Ed Hulbert to assist him in finding some lost pigs. The two men searched and searched and finally found the pigs in a pit. Royal took them home. Hulbert, however, decided to investigate the pit and, upon digging, found ancient hammers, pieces of copper, and decorated carrying baskets.

Apparently Hulbert had known of the pit for perhaps five years or more prior to this incident—if, in fact, the pig story is true. Since the early 1850s he had surveyed extensively throughout the Copper County looking for just the right location to mine. This pig pit looked like the answer. Hulbert requested the directors of the Hulbert Mining Company to form the Calumet Mining Company on September 17, 1864. In November, 1864, he proposed a second company called the Hecla Mining Company, which was also formed. The first shaft of the Hecla Company was sunk on the site of the ancient pit. The Hecla Mining Company paid its first dividend in 1869 and the Calumet followed in 1870. On March 24, 1871, the two companies merged with Alexander Agassiz as president.

Calumet and Hecla prospered with a number of shafts, concentrating plants, and smelters. By the year 1900 it had treated 21 million tons of ore and extracted 1.5 billion pounds of copper, paying dividends totalling $72,250,000. By 1916, C & H was operating at capacity with 11,000 employees. It reorganized in 1923 as the Calumet and Hecla Consolidated Copper Company. After diversifying, the holdings were acquired in April, 1968, by Universal Oil Products, but the following August, a dispute between management and labor produced a strike which closed the mine permanently.

As the copper mines developed, so did the iron mines, with a number of similarities. The severe winters often isolated the mining towns, leaving them without news, supplies and even money. The mining companies resorted to printing their own currency, usually in one, two, five, and ten dollar units. It became known as "iron" or "copper" money and was widely accepted.

Early housing was provided by the companies at low monthly rates as an inducement to recruit and hold workers. Some companies operated stores, while others built stores and leased them out as a concession. Many of the companies organized hospitals including the Calumet and Hecla Mining Company which had theirs built by 1868, even before the mine had paid its first dividend. In many cases, a small amount of money, usually under $1, was deducted from a miner's monthly wage to help pay for doctors, medicines, and sometimes even death benefits.

While copper was known and recovered by the ancients, there seemed to be little general knowledge of iron ore. William Austin Burt and his surveying party discovered the first iron ore in the Lake Superior region of what is now Michigan, Wisconsin, Minnesota, and Ontario. The first mining company to work in the area was the Jackson Mining Company of Jackson, Michigan, which organized

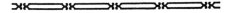

The Copper Range Dock and Railroad, top left, were photographed in 1909. The center photograph of the Calumet and Hecla Ahmeek Mine was taken about 1920. The hoist house is visible on the left, the head frame is on the right. At bottom left is a view of the Cliffs-Shaft Mine as it looked in October, 1955.

29

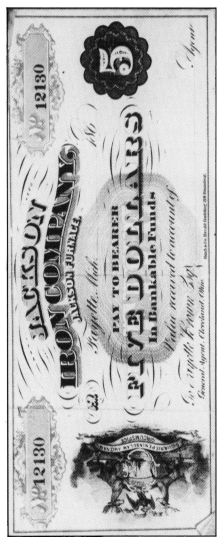

photo courtesy of Cleveland-Cliffs

Pictured above is unused iron money, issued by the Jackson Iron Company about 1860. The monument above right was erected by that company in October, 1904, to mark the first discovery of iron ore in the Lake Superior region. It reads, in part, "The ore was found under the roots of a fallen pine tree in June 1845 by Marji Gesick, a Chief of the Chippewa Tribe of Indians. The land was secured by a mining 'permit' and the property subsequently developed by the Jackson Mining Company organized July 23, 1845."

photo by Homburg, courtesy of Cleveland-Cliffs

in 1845 and sent a group of explorers, led by Philo Everett, to the Upper Peninsula. They followed the Indian trail from Lake Superior to Teal Lake and met Marji Gesick, the local chief. Gesick took them to the area just west of Burt's discovery and showed them pieces of high-grade hard iron ore. Within a short time, the site became the location of the first iron mine—the Jackson Mine.

The Cleveland Mining Company, which was predecessor to the Cleveland-Cliffs Iron Company, was organized in November, 1847. Beginning in 1890 under the direction of William Gwinn Mather, the company pioneered social programs, pension plans, multilingual safety rule books, extended family health care, and several other employee-oriented benefits. Mather also established the Cliffs "open land policy." The company operated several successful mines, including the Cliffs Shaft Mine which had the longest record of production in the Lake Superior region.

The early iron mining companies did not intend to ship iron ore. Their plan was to smelt pig iron, using charcoal made from the Upper Peninsula's abundant hardwoods. The Lake Superior region's first iron was produced on February 10, 1848.

The success of the iron and copper mines put pressure on Congress to do something about navigation into Lake Superior. Because of the rapids at Sault Ste. Marie, personnel and supplies had to be portaged which required changing vessels. After much debate, the construction of a set of shipping locks at Sault Ste. Marie was completed by April, 1855. The Cleveland Iron Mining Company sent the first major iron ore shipment from Marquette in August, 1855, destined for the Crawford and Price wharf in Cleveland, Ohio. By the Civil War, the Marquette Range was shipping at a substantial rate per year, giving a significant advantage to the North.

Iron ore was found in what is now Iron River by the federal surveyors in 1851. However, the area remained undeveloped for several years. Completion of a railroad from Escanaba to Norway-Vulcan led to the opening of the Menominee Range in 1872. In 1884, the Gogebic Range was opened and, though last to be developed, it rapidly became a major producer on both the Michigan and Wisconsin sides of the Montreal River.

photo courtesy of Cleveland Cliffs

photo courtesy of Cleveland-Cliffs

Except for the shallow pits of the ancients and some prospecting for copper, the bulk of the copper mine production came from underground operations. By contrast, the early iron mines were open pit operations, and in some cases, the railroads came right into the pits. As the operations went deeper into the open pits, inclined or vertical "skip-roads" were built in which the skips—big buckets or cars—were operated from hoists on the surface. Great quantities of timber were required for ground support in both the copper and iron mines, which led to the suggestion that "the best forests of Michigan are underground."

The early miners drilled their blast holes by hand. Usually, one man held the drill steel in his hand while his partner struck it with a hammer. The cutting face of the drill was chisel-like so the holder of the steel would rotate it after each blow to keep the hole as round as possible. The two-man team was called "single-jacking". If two men struck alternately while a third held and rotated the steel, it was called "double-jacking." Quite often a lad's first job consisted of bringing the drill steel to the miners. His second job was to hold the steel. It was the ultimate test of confidence!

Dramatic changes took place in mining and milling equipment during the 1870s. There were bigger pumps, stamps, and hoists, and in 1879, Quincy Mining Company introduced the first telephones underground. The Michigan College of Mines, later renamed Michigan Technological University, was established in Houghton in 1885. Also in the 1870s and 1880s, the railroad and telegraph systems expanded, aiding both the mineral and the forest products industries. By the 1880s, as much as 90 percent of all United States' copper, and more than 40 percent of its iron ore were coming from Michigan's Upper Peninsula.

The years of World War II saw record production levels from the underground iron mines—eventually depleting some of them and reaching depths in others that made profitable operations more difficult. With intensive metallurgical research, such methods as froth flotation and pelletizing were developed to boost mining capacities. But the end was in sight. The Gogebic Range was, in 1967, the first to close down completely. The Menominee Range

The photo above shows iron mining at the Jackson Mine in Negaunee about 1860. Look for the man dressed in a white coat. He's the mining captain. The iron miners, above left, are drilling blast holes by hand in a three-person process called double-jacking.

photo courtesy of Cleveland Cliffs

photo courtesy of Cleveland-Cliffs

The row of company houses for workers of the Salisbury Mine in Ishpeming, above, was photographed about 1897. Note the neatly fenced back yards and outdoor privies. The center photograph shows the Negaunee Mine's #1 and #2 shafts around 1890. The Pioneer Furnace in Negaunee, at right, operated during the 1880s. It was the first blast furnace used in the Lake Superior region.

photo courtesy of Cleveland-Cliffs

photo courtesy of Delta County Historical Society

photo courtesy of Cleveland-Cliffs

closed its last underground mine in August, 1978.

The visitor today can see many monuments to the copper and iron miners. Among them is the Cornish Pump in Iron Mountain, built in 1893. It could pump 3,400 gallons of water per minute from a depth of 1500 feet. The flywheel is 40 feet in diameter and the pump stands 54 feet above its foundation. There is also the Quincy Mine Number 2 Shafthouse and Hoist House tower—the world's largest steam-powered mine hoist which has been preserved by the Quincy Mine Hoist Association. Throughout the Upper Peninsula there are numerous excellent mining museums and historical societies with collections of mining memorabilia that bring the era of candle lamps and hand-held drills back to life.

I will never forget my own years working underground—with all the sights, smells and sounds; the darkness and the light; the camaraderie of fellow workers, and the loneliness of solitary mining, while singing the old favorite songs with varying acoustics. In putting down the pen, I am reminded of the two retired miners sitting on a bench, looking into the sunset. Says one, "Partner, things ain't like they used to be!" His friend replies, "No, Jan, and never was!" Then too, there were the words of my old friend and sage, Ernie Allen, who once said, "The good old days were awful!"

By the end of 1982, the three iron ranges had produced and shipped the following amounts: Marquette 529,275,750 long tons; Menominee 324,812,925 long tons; Gogebic 255,224,103 long tons; for a total of 1,109,312,778 long tons. The billionth ton was shiped in 1975 and a second billion tons appears possible.

These figures do not include charcoal iron. It is estimated that between 1848 and 1898, more than 1.8 million tons of charcoal iron were produced and shipped.

The total copper production through 1982 amounted to 10,520,218,094 pounds of native copper and 2,825,305,792 pounds of copper from sulfide ores, for a total of 13,345,523,886 pounds.

Pictured above is the steel head frame of "D" shaft at the East Norrie Mine in Ironwood. The ore dock, above left, was photographed around 1870.

photo by Childs Art Gallery, courtesy of Superior View

34

STRIKE!

During the latter part of the Nineteenth Century, Upper Peninsula copper mine managers became aware of a growing unrest among their workers. The labor movements in the industrial centers of the nation were slowly making an impact in the north, where workers were taking steps to organize unions. While strikes against mining companies prior to the turn of the century were too weak to cause much disruption to company production, they did indicate an underlying dissatisfaction in working conditions. Laborers also suspected that mining companies were making high profits and they wanted a share of them. Many of the mining companies were gradually taking steps to aid the workers. For example, long before the state and federal government welfare systems were created to help injured workers, several mining companies had established aid funds to provide assistance to employees. In 1872, the Calumet and Hecla Mining Company set up one of the earliest of such foundations in the United States. But many workers believed that companies took such steps primarily because they feared the consequences of having an outside labor union represent their work force—not because of their concern for the worker.

One of the first labor unions which attempted to penetrate the Upper Peninsula mine regions and organize both skilled and unskilled workers was the Knights of Labor. Begun as a secret society in 1869, the Knights of Labor grew rapidly and by 1885 it had a membership of more than 700,000. It also declined rapidly as a result of poor leadership, although not before it had gained a foothold in two Copper Country foundries in 1887.

Calumet and Hecla Mining Company officials worked to set up a company-run union to counteract outside organizing forces, and the Knights were not strong enough to sustain their hold. In early 1891, a successful drive was launched by the mining companies to eliminate whatever vestiges of the Knights of Labor remained. Officials then discharged any workers who had joined the union *"as fast as any breach of our regulations or their contracts or duties gives the occasion."* If that method was too slow, the miner's involvement with the union was often considered adequate grounds for dismissal. The harsh stand against unionization came back to haunt the companies but, for awhile, many local groups were supportive of keeping outsiders out.

As the Knights of Labor became ineffective, more militant groups took up the challenge of organizing the miners. At the same

A photographer from the Childs Art Gallery shot this photo of the Ishpeming Mine strike in 1895.

time, a national economic depression hit the mine fields, causing layoffs which further strained relations between mining companies and their workers. During 1894, several workers were injured in the iron mining regions of the U.P. when they tried to interfere with company operations. The iron workers had been seeking wage increases based upon contracts for the amount of ore raised in 1895. After their request was dismissed by management, the miners decided to initiate a general walkout in the Marquette region. They organized an independent local union and had a strike underway by summer. Parades in support of the walkout filled the streets with bands and banners, and marchers totalled several thousand men and women. As the strike wore on, the companies offered wage increases but resisted recognition of a labor union. To counter the refusal of workers to return to their jobs, the mining companies began importing outside workers as strikebreakers.

One of the weaknesses of the workers' movement was the division among them as to the priorities of their demands. Some wanted only higher pay—others were also insisting on union recognition. The division in goals began to take its toll and by early fall, the strike ended. The miners returned to work on company terms and the union was not recognized as the official bargaining agent. Conditions on the Marquette iron range gradually improved, but the discontent from lack of official union recognition continued.

The Western Federation of Miners was organized in 1893, and it blazed a path of violence in mining camps across the country. Collision was inevitable when the tough, uncompromising frontiersmen met the harsh power of the employers head-on. The resulting violence eventually engulfed even the remote mining regions of the Upper Peninsula which, during the 1890s, were experiencing significant growth. New immigrants from northern and central Europe brought a more socialistic attitude that supported the labor movement and further inflamed the mining camps. The mining companies resented the impact of this foreign doctrine, but they needed the labor that the workers provided. Mining company officials thought the new workers should appreciate company generosity in providing homes, schools, hospitals, land for gardens and pastures, and churches and libraries. But unionization attempts with occasional violence continued. From 1890 to 1900, labor unrest resulted in serious production losses because of the frequent strikes and work stoppages. The losses were not severe enough to stop company operations altogether, but the stage was being set for more serious encounters.

It was in Rockland, at the Michigan Mine, that a Finnish-speaking union organizer so inflamed the audience on the sad working conditions at the mine that within a month, a majority of the Finnish workers walked out on strike. Tension grew rapidly until violence broke out resulting in the deaths of a striker and a deputy. Mass arrests were made and private property was ransacked looking for more suspects. More than 100 Finns were jailed on charges of disturbing the peace. The wide coverage given to the Rockland uprising helped bring national attention to the working conditions in the peninsula's mine fields.

The Western Federation of Miners drew many of the immigrant workers into its ranks, and organized the miners with

photo courtesy of Superior View, Marquette

photo by Childs Art Gallery, courtesy of Superior View, Marquette

photo by J.W. Nara, courtesy of Superior View, Marquette

The Finns in the top photograph were striking against what they believed to be Communist intervention. The miners' parade at center was held in Negaunee in 1895. Fearing that violence might erupt during a strike, the National Guard was often called in to help keep the peace. Several of the armed guardsmen gathered to pose, left, for photographer J.W. Nara.

photo by J.W. Nara, courtesy of Superior View, Marquette

cooperation from the International Workers of the World. The IWW was a rival union of the WFM, and even more class conscious. The Preamble of the IWW stated, *"The working class and employing class have nothing in common...a struggle must go on until the workers of the world organize as a class, take possession of the earth, and the machinery of production, and abolish the wage system. It is the historic mission of the working class to do away with capitalism."* Into the copper and iron fields of the Upper Peninsula marched these organizers. In spite of often having government support on their side, the mine owners feared and felt greatly threatened by these angry, violent groups.

By 1908, the Western Federation of Miners was sending in union organizers to meet with local labor leaders and plan a strategy against the mine managers. The copper mines at this time were prospering, reaching peaks on the stock market and paying out high dividends. One such mining company was reported to be paying a one-dollar dividend for each dollar paid in wages. This flush period was short-lived, however, as the mine managers soon had to contend with declining ore grades and higher operating costs. Wages were cut, which resulted in the wages of U.P. copper miners being only half the hourly rates of those in the Montana copper mines. Such differences fueled the WFM leaders' organizing efforts, which continued with great zeal and success.

Four years of the WFM's struggle to unite workers eventually paid off, setting the stage for the 1913 copper miners' strike. The workers wanted: (1) a shorter work day, eight hours instead of twelve; (2) a new minimum wage; (3) better working conditions including abandonment of the dangerous one-man drill; and (4) recognition of the union as the local bargaining agent. The mining companies rejected the demands and placed the blame on outside agitators for the discontent of the workers.

From the national unions came such organizers as Charles Moyer, Martin Hendrickson, Mary (Mother Jones) Harris, Frank Little and John Mitchell. Although some only put in brief appearances, several made their mark and gave local union leaders support to conduct what was hoped to be a very successful labor

This dramatic scene took place when a caravan of horse-drawn hearses carried away the bodies of 74 people who had been killed in the panic at the Calumet Italian Hall Christmas party. More than 50 of the victims were children.

38

strike. But success was not to come easily for organized labor.

In the spring of 1913, an ominous cloud was moving over the copper range of the Keweenaw Peninsula. Rumors of a strike were everywhere, and workers were uncomfortable, but the WFM leadership reassured the men of outside support. There was strong talk among the union membership that the mining companies were making plans to bolster their watch force in the event a strike did take place. The local news media, although still strongly pro-company, now had new competition from several foreign language newspapers such as the pro-labor *Tyomies* publication. Worker demands were being discussed by local representatives in the state legislature in hopes of avoiding a confrontation between organized labor and the mining companies. But it was not to be.

In July, local union leaders were still wondering if they would receive help from the national organization. Although some of the more radical members wanted to call the strike quickly, the local officers waited for word from Charles Moyer, president of the WFM. The union locals polled their membership, and the result was a vote of 70 to 1 favoring a strike if the mining company did not meet worker demands. The company rejected the demands and, on July 23, 1913, the strike began. With permission from the Houghton County Board of Supervisors, the sheriff arranged for armed deputies to come from the Waddell-Mahon Agency of New York. These specially trained security men were brought in to protect company property, but they caused great agitation among the strikers who viewed them as strikebreakers. Tension mounted, and Governor Woodbridge Ferris sent in the National Guard with instructions to protect life and property, and to preserve order.

There were many casualties of that famous strike. Reputations were ruined, churches were divided, families split, businesses were boycotted, and lives were lost. The bloodshed of a street duel, the arson of a store in Centennial, the shooting of two strikers near Painesdale, the killing of a young girl in Calumet, the dynamiting of a company building in Ahmeek and a passenger train in Keweenaw, and the murders of imported strikebreakers were followed by one of the greatest tragedies to hit the Upper Peninsula. On Christmas Eve of 1913, a holiday party was underway in the Italian Hall in Calumet when someone yelled, "Fire!" There was no fire, but before that was known, panic overtook the crowd. The doors of the hall opened inward, preventing an easy exodus, and in the stampede to get outside, seventy-four people were killed including more than fifty children who were crushed in the stairwell. It was never learned who caused the senseless tragedy. Further violence followed, including the shooting of union president Charles Moyer.

Churches, too, were caught up in the labor strife, especially between 1913-14. In the English-speaking church community parishioners took a more passive role because many of the church leaders were from company management ranks. Some union leaders felt the local Methodist Church showed very little sympathy for the strikers and the hardship of the families. They said that the local Methodist Ministerial Association "timidly equivocated and straddled the issues as had other churchmen." It was even rumored that if a person wanted a good job at the mining company, they had better have a good singing voice and be a member of the Methodist

photo courtesy of Superior View, Marquette

One of the 1913 Copper Country strike heroines was, above, Annie Clemenc. Below is a 1913 Circuit Court injunction filed by The Baltic Mining Company against the Western Federation of Miners.

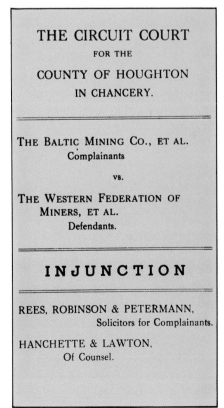

THE CIRCUIT COURT
FOR THE
COUNTY OF HOUGHTON
IN CHANCERY.

THE BALTIC MINING CO., ET AL.
Complainants

vs.

THE WESTERN FEDERATION OF
MINERS, ET AL.
Defendants.

INJUNCTION

REES, ROBINSON & PETERMANN,
Solicitors for Complainants.

HANCHETTE & LAWTON,
Of Counsel.

photo from the Jack Foster collection

photo from the Jack Foster Collection

photo from Michigan Technological University Library Archives

Miners such as those in the top photo went on strike for a variety of reasons including better pay, shortened work days, safer working conditions, and union recognition. During the 1913 strikes, the guardsmen in the center and bottom photos were called in to protect life and property, and to preserve order.

photo by J.W. Nara, courtesy of Superior View, Marquette

40

Society. The Catholic Churches were considered pro-labor, but priests did not expound on the issue, at least from the pulpit. Some of their publications, however, did express strong feelings against mine management after interviews with strikers and union labor leaders detailed the difficulties of worker lives. The strongest divisions persisted among Lutheran congregations.

The pastor of Pine Street Church of Calumet, the Rev. A.L. Heideman, was quite vocal in support of the labor movement and made no apology for it. When some of the mining company officials suggested to the minister that it would be proper to encourage the workers of his congregation to ignore the strike and return to work, it so incensed him that he promptly invited the labor organizer John Korpi to speak to his congregation from the pulpit.

The 1913 copper miners' strike lasted nine months, and the real losers were the miners. Many became disillusioned and left the region to work in the automobile factories in Detroit. Others struck out to find employment in the western regions of the country.

Although mining companies tried to deny that they discriminated against miners who participated in the strike, it was well-known that for years afterwards blacklists were used to rid companies of union troublemakers and their families.

Labor disputes soon rippled into the western United States' copper mines, sending some of the miners back to the U.P. in 1916-17. The mining companies, wary of troublesome union organizers, often ran suspicious characters out of town. The IWW and the WFM were defeated in Michigan, Minnesota, and even the West. The loss of more than 5,000 men from the mining district to the armed forces in World War I, and many thousands more to Detroit and other industrial centers, created a serious shortage of labor in the U.P. Even with a wage increase in late 1918, there still wasn't enough labor to help the ailing copper industry. Only after the Armistice did the work force become adequate.

Wages for copper industry workers in 1919 were about $3.76 per day, although the iron industry had already reached $6.28 per day. As the peninsula entered the 1920s, copper mining was weakening and moving into a twenty-year phase of decline from which it would never recover. While lower grade copper mines were shutting down, the iron mining industry had many years of prosperity ahead, and organized labor was gradually gaining a lasting foothold in the mining regions of the western Upper Peninsula.

Logging was a hazardous business and wood workers felt they, too, needed protection. But the peninsula's timber industry experienced few attempts to organize. In fact, the eight-hour day evaded their reach until well into the 1920s. The small size of many lumber camps, the power of a family-run operation, isolation of workers, and the seasonal base of the timber industry, all contributed to the failure of wood workers to gain union recognition.

After fighting the onslaught of organized labor for more than 50 years, collective bargaining became a reality in both the mining and forest industries. The AFL, CIO, Woodworkers, and other unions eventually even gained support from federal legislation designed to protect the rights of workers to organize. Through years of diligent effort, working conditions have been dramatically improved for the industrial base that now exists.

photo courtesy of Ray Maurin

Moonshine On The Gogebic

Mining and logging were notoriously thirsty jobs and there weren't any government laws which could alter that fact. Oh, they could impose restrictions, make arrests and padlock doors, but as long as the thirst was there, it could be satisfied, one way or another. In fact, thirsts on the Michigan side of the Gogebic Range had a considerable edge over those in other Upper Peninsula towns during Prohibition days—an edge called Hurley. Ironwood and Hurley face each other across the East Branch of the Montreal River, the natural and legal boundary between Michigan and Wisconsin. In their early lives, these two communities subsisted on tall timber and deep mines, and because of their industrial, geographic and social similarities it would be difficult to write about one without the other, so tales of both are included in this story.

Iron mining on the Gogebic Range began in the mid-1880s and almost overnight mining camps and communities took root. Typical frontier towns with rough frame buildings, wooden sidewalks and dirt roads were inhabited by immigrants of twenty different nationalities. They arrived from "the old country" to work in the 55 underground mines, in the score of lumber camps, or on the farms which followed the cross-cut saws. In 1905, more than two-thirds of Gogebic County's adult population were foreign born, with Finns, Italians, and Canadians predominating in that order. Surprisingly enough, the Cornish "Cousin Jacks" who reigned supreme in earlier Upper Peninsula mining communities were scarcely noticeable in western Gogebic County.

In those days, miners worked twelve hours a day, six days a week, and their relaxation activities had to be quick and convenient. Fast service saloons and palaces of pleasure seemed the answer to their recreational needs. In Ironwood alone, 31 saloons responded gallantly to social demands. Hurley, with less than half the population of Ironwood, had 51 saloons lined up along the five blocks of Silver Street and all of them kept busy.

Obviously, two towns the size of Hurley and Ironwood couldn't possibly support 82 saloons, but with streetcar tracks tying them to other small communities in Michigan and Wisconsin, there were few empty places at the bar. When evening establishments and feminine attractions became more lavish, they began drawing clientele from the big cities to the south, many of whom stayed at the luxurious Burton House in Hurley. Boasting a hundred elegant rooms and prestigious service, the Burton hosted many prominent

Ironwood and Hurley face each other across the Michigan-Wisconsin line and, at the turn of the century, the two towns had a total of more than 80 saloons. When Michigan banned the Sunday sale of alcohol, thirsty miners and loggers would take the streetcar just across the state line and continue their favorite pastime.

photo courtesy of Superior View, Marquette

people including President Grover Cleveland and novelist Edna Ferber. The records don't disclose Cleveland's mission in Hurley, but Ferber was researching the murder of Lottie Morgan, a popular Hurley prostitute whose life and death were later depicted in the best-selling novel and movie *Come And Get It.*

Long before Prohibition temporarily inconvenienced dusty tonsils along the Gogebic Range, Michigan laws had banned the Sunday sale of alcohol. Fortunately, the interstate streetcar was a lifeline to a more lenient Wisconsin, and *their* bars had standing room only on that day of rest. However, when the 18th amendment was adopted in 1919 and total Prohibition cast a pall over elbow-benders everywhere, Hurley and Ironwood faced the crisis together. Of the two, Hurley was far more successful in maintaining its status as a fun-loving community, for tavern keepers simply chose to ignore that Prohibition stuff, there being a universal feeling that they lived north of the law. Oh, they made an occasional outward sign of compliance from time to time and indeed, there were a few patrons who sipped a glass of "near-beer," that being the only legal beverage that even sounded like fun. But generally speaking, the huge reserve of real stuff stockpiled before Prohibition was served

"Revenuers" combed Gogebic Range back roads during Prohibition looking for violators of the law. Pictured above, the six bottles of clear liquid set up on the car's running board might indicate that these agents found some evidence. It looks like the deputies at right set out to break up someone's still, and did a pretty good job of it.

photo courtesy of Superior View, Marquette

44

with a wink to anyone who professed to know "Joe."

Federal agents who were assigned to the enforcement of the 18th amendment were not particularly amused with Hurley's eye-winking attitude toward the law, and they found even less humor in the river of booze which continued to flow upstream from Milwaukee to Hurley and Ironwood. The hide-and-seek games between federal agents and whiskey merchants, which had continued rather quietly during the first year of Prohibition, erupted into gunfire on the evening of October 20, 1920.

For weeks, a group of Ironwood and Hurley men, along with John Filion from Marquette, had been organizing a 21-car expedition to run a supply of good bonded booze from Milwaukee to the Gogebic Range taverns. It was the last time the locals would trust an outsider, for Filion was actually a federal agent. Other agents waiting along the route were able to pick off the two rear vehicles and 130 cases of whiskey near Woodruff. Then they quickly established a roadblock for the remainder of the caravan just north of Mercer. The two lead cars attempted to run the blockade but one bogged down on the sandy shoulder and the other swerved to an abrupt halt when its driver, Joe Chiapusio, was shot in the back with a rifle. The remaining 17 cars in the caravan responded to the gunfire with a batch of tire-squealing turnabouts and continued on to Hurley and Ironwood via a network of backwoods roads.

Up until the time Joe slumped over the wheel, it had been a typical cat-and-mouse episode, little different from dozens of others which had taken place previously. Catching whiskey runners and pouring their booze in the ditch was one thing...killing a local man was quite another. In fact, there was an air of mystery to the entire federal operation. No move was made to assist the wounded man and the agents did not inform local authorities of their plans. They simply deputized a passing motorist to take the mortally wounded Chiapusio to the Ironwood hospital, then left the scene. To add to the intrigue, Chiapusio, who died shortly after entering the hospital, was found to have sold a vehicle to Filion just prior to the Milwaukee expedition.

A coroner's inquest determined that the shooting was unjustified, and charges were brought against six federal officers, including Arthur Scully, the man who fired the fatal shot. However, the coroner's jury and the Iron County district attorney were powerless to bring those charged back into Wisconsin from their home states of Michigan and Illinois.

The episode did not disrupt the flow of spirits into the Gogebic Range, and caravans continued their northerly migrations with eagerly-awaited cargoes. Despite the combined efforts of state and federal enforcement officers, the supply lines remained so effective that agents decided to concentrate on closing the outlets on the northern end of the route. On December 28, 1920, they made their move. Sixty federal men from Chicago descended on Hurley, armed with warrants issued by Judge Kennesaw Mountain Landis and a determination to close the town. Within an hour, fifty-seven saloon keepers and bartenders were arrested for liquor violations and carted off to the federal building in Ashland. Bail was set at $1500 for saloon owners and $1000 for bartenders. As each individual was processed, his bond was paid by friends and relatives and he was

photo courtesy of Menominee Range Museum, Iron Mountain

soon back in Hurley. Local feelings ran heavily in favor of those who quenched thirsts, and assuming that an unbiased trial in the Gogebic area would be highly improbable, authorities selected LaCrosse, Wisconsin as an alternate site.

The case was undecided for more than two years. Finally, in the spring of 1923, a federal grand jury in Madison determined that warrants used in the 1920 raid were illegal, and charges against the 57 men were dismissed. During the interim, of course, business had continued as usual along Silver Street. Saloons were intermittently raided and closed throughout the Prohibition era but, with such minimal local support, efforts to really close down Hurley were pretty futile. Most of these arrests and token closures were less than spectacular, but a March 1927 raid on Silver Street saloons was somewhat notable in that the town marshall had to make a mid-raid purchasing trip to Ironwood because the Hurley hardware store ran out of padlocks. Padlocks sold well during Prohibition.

Keeping Hurley in motion was as important to the community's treasury as it was to the saloon-keepers' bank accounts and the miners' thirsts. When Dominic Rubatt was elected mayor in 1926, the city treasury was almost empty, but the good mayor came up with a plan for improving the budget. Working with city attorney Everis Reid and county judge James Flandrena, the mayor imposed a fine of $275 on each of the 44 saloon operators, which had to be paid before their licenses would be considered for renewal. They all appeared in court, pleaded guilty and paid their fines with a universal belief that doing so entitled them to operate as they darn pleased. It did—and they did!

If saloons, prostitution and gambling could be a panacea for community financial woes, Mayor Rubatt reasoned that they just might benefit a hard-working public official as well. With this in mind, he became the new co-owner of Joe Raineri's grocery store and immediately began specializing in corn sugar, receiving it in carload shipments. Being the popular base for moonshine mash, it sold very well, indeed.

Anton Bialecke was born in 1902 and spent 47 years as a blacksmith in the Anvil Mine, beginning as an apprentice at the age of fourteen. He readily admitted that he was a darned good blacksmith, but confessed that making moonshine was not one of

Some home-brewing operations were pretty sophisticated, as this one appears to be.

photo courtesy of Superior View, Marquette

his talents. "I knew a lot of them who did, though, and some of it was darn good, you betcha! There were four lids on most of the old kitchen wood stoves—two for cooking food, and two for heating the stills. They made moonshine out of apples, prunes and grapes, and if it was a little strong, they'd water it to taste before jugging it. Damn, there were a lot of blind pigs in Bessemer—but no more than any other town on the Gogebic Range, I guess."

Ted Hulstrom of Ironwood recalled that "Slim" Willis used to make moonshine in the woods, transporting it to town by hiding it in the same wagonload of wood all year long. "One day, some men asked me where Slim's wood operation was and without thinking, I told them. They were feds and Slim got sent up because of my big mouth and I felt real bad about that!"

A retired Ironwood telephone man recalled that during Prohibition he frequently installed cables above stills which were perking away. "Once, I had to come down every few minutes because the fumes were giving me a snootful."

Rita Schumm from Ironwood recalled that her father crossed the Montreal River to a small house near the railroad tracks to pick up his liquor. One of the bootleggers involved went blind one day—"Not from drinking his own moonshine, but from standing too close when the still blew up!"

Wine was another do-it-yourself thirst-quencher and after the first and second runs of wine were bottled, the residue—which included seeds, stems and whatever fell in—was boiled to make grapa.

"One time we were out at a camp in the bush and John Kajala got really drunk on grapa," recalls Fred Tezak. "They poured a water glass full for me but when I saw what looked like fog winding around in the half-empty jug, I took the first chance I had to spill mine behind a tree. When John finally folded up, the boys wrapped his whole head in bandages, except his nose, and when he came to, they told him he had fallen off the wagon head-first and hit a stump. The way he felt, he had no reason to doubt them!"

Leonard Michaelson, a retired Ironwood man, had more than a casual interest in the welfare of Gogebic saloons. "Saloons used to sell good Canadian whiskey for twenty-five dollars a quart in 1924," he recalled, "and I hauled lots of it in a brand new Oakland sedan...paid for the car in three months! We picked up booze from

This is the inside of Hurley's Marble Hall Bar. Notice the ever-present spittoons.

photo courtesy of Ironwood Historical Museum

photo courtesy of Ironwood Historical Museum

Gogebic Range loggers, such as those in the top photo, worked and played hard—so the stories go. They helped keep the saloons and bootleggers of Ironwood and Hurley in business, even during Prohibition. At center, many of these dedicated workers of the Number 2 Norrie Mine in Ironwood no doubt poured down their share of whiskey and moonshine during the Gogebic Range's glory days. Busting bootleggers was serious work and sometimes the police were called in to help. The photograph of the Michigan State Police with a big haul of confiscated moonshine and stills, at right, was taken in the 1920s.

photo courtesy of Superior View, Marquette

48

Hurley. Cary and Pence and I would bring it to one central point in Ironwood—Fucello usually handled it from there. We always had girlfriends with us and it was kind of fun—except the time we got hijacked and lost the whole works. Everyone on the Range made their own home brew. We'd check each other's recipes and try them out. The Belgians made beer with hops, barley, and raisins for extra kick. They had one problem—they made their beer so fast, it never had a chance to develop a decent head. They'd take care of that by adding beaten egg white to every bottle. Now *there* was a head!

"The lumberjacks would come into Hurley when the logging season was over, and Silver Street girls, gambling, and whiskey would take care of their stake in short order. The saloon operators would then give them one free drink, kick them out, and they'd sit along the sunny side of Silver Street wondering how they'd eat until the logging camps reopened. Most often, the cops would pick them up for loitering, and they'd be sentenced to clean up the *goldarn* town for a couple weeks or serve time at the work camp at Manitowish. But it was a darn sight easier work than they were used to and it beat wandering around with a hungry stomach." Michaelson remembered that Judge Griff Thomas, who presided in Iron County during 1920-23, never discriminated against the lumberjacks...or anyone else, for that matter. According to Michaelson, Judge Thomas could neither read nor write, but he could turn over a page in his log and say, "That'll cost you twenty dollars." He was real good at that.

One lumberjack friend of Michaelson was awarded $20,000 from the Scott and Howe sawmill for having a hand ground off by a faulty saw. It was a questionable gain, however, because he invested his money in a big still in north Ironwood and in no time at all became his own best customer. Between his unquenchable thirst and the great sums of hush money paid to local authorities, his business collapsed, and he held himself a private hanging in a little W.P.A. shack on the edge of town. On the Gogebic Range, Prohibition was not all bubbles, laughter and song.

Andy Bednar admits to being one of the youngest bootleggers in town because his mother was sure that nobody would bother a little boy pulling a box on a sleigh. "It wasn't too bad when I was buying just for the family," he muses, "but the neighbors usually knew when I was going, and when they placed their orders, sometimes that box was pretty full!"

The market for corn sugar has long since disappeared on the Gogebic Range. The painted ladies no longer predominate on downtown sidewalks, and the bars along Silver Street are mere shadows of their ancestors. The Burton House burned in 1947, the last mine closed in 1966, and the populations of Ironwood, Hurley and neighboring towns have dwindled. Many of the events on the Gogebic Range during the Roaring Twenties were pretty humorous, and those are the stories which are best remembered and repeated. Today's western Upper Peninsula old folks are far less inclined to dwell on the murders, public graft, white slavery, and almost total lack of business ethics which were routine throughout Prohibition. It's probably a good thing, for who would believe them?

Editor's note: At the request of Gogebic Range folks who shared stories with the author, some of the names have been changed.

photo courtesy of Bruce Deter, Arvon

The $2,000,000 Ride

Ever get that letdown feeling when your raffle number doesn't come crashing through a winner, when a three-buck household gimmick produces $7 worth of chores, or your bargain waders part on the downstream side when you're netting an upstream brook trout? Read on—then kiss thanks to your favorite rabbit's foot that you weren't around to risk a little green on the Iron Range and Huron Bay Railroad back in 1890. Many did, thanks to Milo Davis, a slick Detroit promoter who convinced all listeners that a Champion to Huron Bay railroad would line their pockets—providing they first emptied them to make room.

On the surface (and most railroads are) the project did look good. In an area already established as one of the country's foremost iron ranges and just a few hours' crow-fly east of the equally famous Copper Country, it didn't take much to convince the flat-landers that the Huron Mountains which lay between were also oozing with mineral wealth. There were also great timber stands waiting patiently to be transported to the mills. And there was the Arvon Quarry—Milo's real convincer. The three slate quarries in operation had already shipped thousands of squares of shingles for roofs in Detroit, Chicago, Milwaukee, and other Midwest cities. E.E. Myers, noted Detroit architect and construction superintendent on the new Capitol building in Lansing, had reported that Huron Bay slate was superior in quality, strength, and durability. The market was there, the product seemed to be unlimited in supply, and the company's 3-foot by 4-mile horse-drawn tram system to the Huron Bay docks was ripe for replacement by a first-class railroad.

Working in reverse on Milo Davis' logical arguments in favor of this wildcat enterprise, we find that from 1890 to 1895 quarrying and track-laying proceeded at about the same pace—in different directions. It was uphill all the way for the railroad construction crews but, thanks to the 1893 depression, increased costs of quarrying and a changing public mind, it was a downhill slide for the Arvon quarry. Both projects finished in a dead heat. In addition, almost all of the iron ore from the Marquette Range was being shipped out of Marquette and Escanaba via the South Shore and the Chicago & Northwestern Railroads, and ore docks already constructed at L'Anse and St. Ignace were just standing around twiddling their pilings. The Chicago, Milwaukee & St. Paul Railroad had enough smarts to stand clear of Milo Davis and Company.

At left, workers are cutting through the rock to lay track for the short-lived Iron Range & Huron Bay Railroad.

But, there was a railroad...sort of. After some big money from Detroit was assured, the articles of incorporation for the Iron Range and Huron Bay Railroad were filed in July, 1890, and work started at once. Milo Davis originally stated that the railroad would be 35 miles long and would cost about $525,000 to construct. He was, however, a little conservative in his estimate—about seven miles and 1½ million dollars conservative, to be precise.

With Milo Davis in charge as able chief engineer and superintendent, the construction program whipped along just about as fast as you might expect it would, having read this far. When the picks and shovels got warmed up in July, Milo predicted that the railroad would be completed before winter set in. For once he was right—partly. He had the correct season but he was five years short on the remainder of the completion date.

Before that last mile of track into Champion was laid in the summer of '95, the thousand or so laborers who wielded pick, shovel, and wheelbarrow or drove teams through gorge and swamp had quite a time. They did get a little breather during the 1893 depression when frivolous projects such as wildcat railroads lay dormant—and some of the crew became even more dormant when typhoid fever broke out in the camps along the grade. But betwixt depression and death, it was strictly mosquitoes, swamp, and rock. And what rock! One seven-mile cut with walls up to 60 feet high took wagon loads of black powder, a beaver dam of sweat, a couple of lives, and almost a year to complete.

During the fall of 1890, bids had been taken for the construction of a large ore dock at Huron Bay. By the time the last of the track found its way into Champion, the quarter-million dollar wooden structure had already been waiting around for a couple of years. Two 110 class locomotives—complete with a first-class interlocking plant, twenty flatcars, lorries, and a well-equipped machine

photo courtesy of L'Anse Township Hall, L'Anse

shop—were chomping at their cow-catchers for the first payload as the long-awaited completion day drew near.

Sam Beck, former Champion hotel operator and a railroad watchman at the time of the first test run, described the experience: "As the last eleven miles of the road were downgrade, we decided the uphill run from Huron Bay would be a good test. I was in the cab with the engineer and we had proceeded just a short distance up the grade when the roadbed gave way and we went into a ditch. From that moment on, the Iron Range and Huron Bay Railroad ceased to exist as a railroad!"

It was decided at this late date that the terrific grades, which were 8 percent in some sections, would be impossible to negotiate unless each car had its own locomotive. It was also about then that the Iron Range and Huron Bay Railroad Company went under financially.

Shortly thereafter, Milo Davis came up with the novel idea of an extended trip into Mexico, thus avoiding the distasteful lawsuits initiated by numerous creditors, employees, and investors. He also avoided the degradation of seeing his entire dream—including tracks, equipment, right-of-way, real estate, bridges, and ore dock—go on the block for $110,000.

Although the Iron Range and Huron Bay never hosted a train over its entire length or hauled a pound of freight, its various components served well in other areas for many years. The steel was used in completing electric lines between Grand Rapids and Holland, Oxford and Flint, and from Romeo to Imlay City. The three million feet of select pine salvaged from the ore dock went for Detroit construction, and the engines found their way north of the Soo to the Algoma Central. Several company buildings near the old dock site remained for years as a tribute to one of the more illustrious flops in the industrial history of the Upper Peninsula. ◄

At left is an Iron Range & Huron Bay locomotive. The map above, taken from the 1897 Michigan Legislative Manual, *shows the never-used route of the IR & HB Railroad running northwest out of Champion, past the Arvon Quarry, and on to Huron Bay.*

photo courtesy of Marion Strahl Boyer

Trains To Everywhere

The first American passenger train appeared in Charleston, South Carolina on Christmas Day, 1830, and it signalled a transformation of this country's lifestyle. The early trains were uncomfortable, slow moving, and unreliable, but the alternate method of travel was a wagon that covered little more than 30 miles in a day. Twenty years after Charleston, powerful engines were moving the trains along at 40-50 miles per hour and making 300-mile trips in a day. Children of all ages had a new hero, the railroad engineer.

Before the advent of trains, most people had lived and died close to their birth place, seldom traveling more than 50 miles from home. But the railroad gave wheels to people and goods, and became a vital part of daily living to an extent difficult to imagine today. The sounds of the train's sharp and rythmic exhaust, and the throaty, resonant whistle carried for miles across the countryside on still nights, and provided comforting assurance that the night train was running and all was well.

Passenger traffic rapidly expanded following the Civil War as tracks extended to all parts of the country. There was a fever of construction with communities competing to attract rail companies, and by 1900, the *Official Guide of the Railways* contained an index of some 55,000 stations across the United States, served by more than 1,200 railroads. The number of passenger trains reached a peak after World War I when 20,000 scheduled runs operated daily. Today fewer than one percent of that number remains.

In the Upper Peninsula train travel was at its greatest shortly after the turn of the century, when 14 common carrier railroads offering scheduled freight and passenger service were in operation. The number of passenger trains chuffing into and out of, up and down, and across the peninsula in a 24-hour period was no less than 178. An unbelievable figure, and it doesn't include the many trains on lumber company railroads that served the logging camps. Most of those carried passengers on a casual basis. One of the largest railroads, the Nahma & Northern, operated for more than 40 years on 50 miles of road and 70 miles of track in northeast Delta County. It served 15 lumber camps, and its principal passengers were lumber jacks and deer hunters. Appropriately, its nickname was the "Whiskey Line."

The first railroad in the U.P. was organized to move iron ore from the Negaunee-area mines to the port of Marquette. Named the

Trains were nearly as important to early Upper Peninsula residents as cars are today. They transported people and goods faster and easier than ever before, and they helped tiny, backwoods communities become boom towns. Some locomotives had names—others just had numbers. This was #51.

Iron Mountain Railroad, it was built in 1857 as a replacement for the mule-pulled cart system used on strap railways. In 1859 it became known as the Bay de Noquet & Marquette Railroad, the first in a series of ownership and name changes that eventually led to its becoming a segment of the Duluth, South Shore & Atlantic Railway (DSS & A.) The new designation was in keeping with the dream of extending the line south to Lake Michigan. The goal wasn't achieved for several years, however, and then it was accomplished by a different group which built from the south toward the ore country.

Gradually expanding through mergers and purchases, the Chicago & North Western Railway (C & NW) reached Ft. Howard, Wisconsin, now called Green Bay, in 1862, on a northerly course from Chicago via Janesville, with an authorization to build northward to the U.P. border. The Civil War was making Upper Peninsula iron ore an increasingly important commodity, and armed with a federal land grant, C & NW president W.B. Ogden decided on a maneuver to bypass the 120 miles separating his track from the closest point on Little Bay De Noc to the Negaunee mines. A subsidiary, the Peninsula Railroad, was formed to build a line from the Jackson Mine to Sand Point, present-day Escanaba, connecting the tracks late in 1864. The first train ran north, powered by a locomotive shipped from Green Bay by scow and unloaded on Christmas Day. The engineer was C.H. Weideman and, in the style of the day, his engine did not have a number but a name; it was called the *Appleton*. The 63-mile line was absorbed by the C & NW. Iron ore began moving over the first of Escanaba's ore docks in 1865, and plans were made to include passenger service. By running horse drawn stages to Escanaba, they began carrying passengers even before the rail line was completed. Scheduled transportation for passengers and mail between Iron Range towns and Green Bay consisted of a combination train and steamer service. The trip from Marquette to Chicago, which began with a

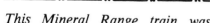

This Mineral Range train was photographed while crossing the Hungarian Falls Trestle.

photo courtesy of Wesley E. Perron, Marquette

train ride on the Bay de Noquet & Marquette to Negaunee, took 33 hours and cost $10.00.

Railroad construction in the U.P. proceeded apace with the increasing demand for copper and lumber, and the opening of mines on the Menominee and Gogebic Iron Ranges. The first construction west from the Negaunee-Ishpeming area reached Champion in 1865, but the 33 miles to L'Anse wasn't bridged until 1872. Houghton was finally reached in 1883 with passenger service from Marquette. The Milwaukee and Northern built north from Green Bay to Iron Mountain in 1888 and extended to a junction with the South Shore at Champion. In 1892, a branch of the line, by then absorbed by the Milwaukee Road, reached Ontonagon from Channing after forming a connection at Sidnaw with the Ontonagon & Brule River Railway. The Milwaukee Road laid track from Kelso Junction to Crystal Falls in 1900, and extended to Iron River in 1914.

The North Western reached the Menominee River from Green Bay in 1871, halfway to its goal of closing the gap to Escanaba. Survey crews first ran lines along the lake shore for the trackage, but with the discovery of iron ore near Quinnesec the route was shifted in that direction, and construction began in both directions toward the town of Powers. By mid-December 1872, the line was completed, connecting with track going to Ishpeming—thus beginning some 97 years of through trains from Ishpeming to Chicago.

Rails were laid to Quinnesec, where iron ore had been discovered, in 1877. In 1880, tracks were laid to Iron Mountain and in 1882 extended to Iron River. By 1887, they were stretched even further west, reaching the Gogebic Range mines. By that time the main line trackage in the U.P. was made up of 300 miles on the North Western and 64 miles on the Marquette & Ontonagon between Marquette and L'Anse.

The eastern part of the Upper Peninsula acquired rail service in 1881 when the Detroit, Mackinac, and Marquette (DM & M) completed the line from St. Ignace to Marquette. Six years later, the

Below is a ticket for the Duluth, South Shore & Atlantic Railway Company showing all the stops from Stoneville to Montreal, and from Sault Ste. Marie to Ishpeming. The bearer of this ticket traveled west between Bruce's Crossing and Watton at a charge of 31 cents. The engine at left is #105 of the South Shore.

photo courtesy of Wesley E. Perron, Marquette

photo from the Frank Bourke collection

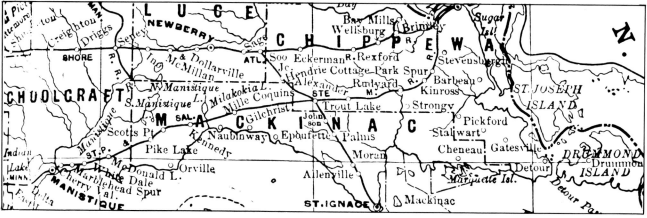

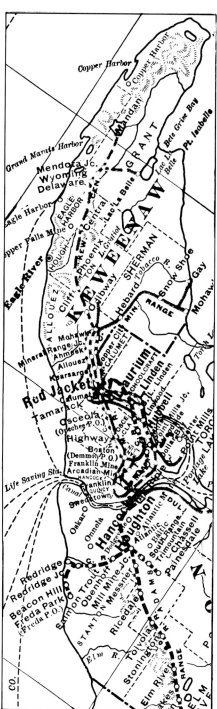

DM & M was bankrupt and taken over by the DSS & A. A branch was built from Soo Junction to the Soo, and on October 6, 1887, passenger service began which, within a year, connected with trains running from St. Ignace to Iron River, Wisconsin and on to Duluth. In December, 1887, the Soo welcomed another railroad when the Soo Line completed 500 miles of track from Minneapolis. A year later, through passenger service to Boston was inaugurated via a connection at the Canadian Soo.

The last of the major lines to build was the Lake Superior & Ishpeming (LS & I) which began in 1896 with 20 miles of track west from Marquette. It later extended north to Big Bay. In 1902, the LS & I built to the southeast, joining with the Munising Railway, which it purchased, at Lawson in Alger County. By 1905 there were 54 daily passenger trains operating over the three Copper Country railroads, and a total of 178 passenger trains across the peninsula. Houghton County's population was 85,000 with a thriving passenger service to match. There were 13 daily departures every day for the 11-mile trip to Lake Linden from Houghton-Hancock, and an equal number leaving for Calumet. Mill Mine Junction was served by 24 daily trains, and passengers had a choice of five departures for Painesdale, three for Redridge and Freda Park, or two that went south to the towns of Greenland and Mass. No train went *through* a station—every one was a scheduled stop. Winona, Toivola, Cole's Creek, Woodside, Linwood, and Grove were just a few of many. Sometimes the stations were only one mile apart!

To the north, the Keweenaw Central operated their 26-mile line from Calumet to Mandan via Kearsarge, Ahmeek, Mohawk, Cliff, Phoenix, Central, and Delaware. In addition to four daily trains, this small line ran several excursion trains to Crest View, a summer resort and casino it owned in Phoenix. This was a grand and busy time for the railroads, and folks could take trains to everywhere.

There were, of course, other busy railroad centers across the peninsula such as at Menominee. Served by the North Western, the Milwaukee, and the Wisconsin & Michigan, the border city saw 26 trains daily. Negaunee and Ishpeming had 21 trains, and Marquette was served by 16 as was Escanaba. Passengers were offered an "all electrically lighted, through palace sleeper" from Chicago to the Soo. At Ironwood, 12 trains arrived and departed daily.

One of the most interesting of the small railroads was the Manistique Railway, affectionately called the "Myrtle Navy" after a popular tobacco of the day. Like most of the others, it began as a

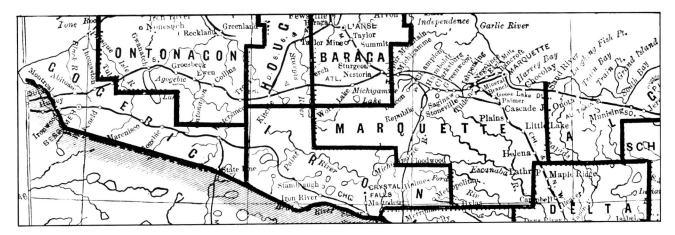

logging road and then enjoyed a thriving common-carrier business during the lumber boom. Beginning with a line from Seney to Grand Marais in 1886, it later built south through Germfask and Curtis to Wilman, connecting with the South Shore at Seney, and the Lake Michigan & Superior at McEwen. In the early 1900s Grand Marais had a population of 3,000, ten times what it is today. In 1906 more than 17,000 paying passengers traveled over its line. Four years later, with the rapid decline of lumbering, the railroad went out of business, but left behind a few historical footprints worth recalling. One young immigrant laborer who worked as a section hand on the Manistique didn't become well known until he drifted away from Seney. In 1901, he showed up in Buffalo where, on September 6, he shot and killed President McKinley. His name was Leon Czolgosz, and in less than two months he was tried, convicted, and electrocuted. There was also Dr. J.P. Bohn of Newberry, who later became a Congressman. Dr. Bohn had made an unusual arrangement with the railroad. They provided him with a locomotive to use for making house calls up and down the line.

Archaeologists of the future may be puzzled to discover a spot where a railroad is located underneath Highway 77. It seems that tracks were built through swampy country, and to fill in one bad sink-hole, thousands of feet of white pine logs were dumped in an effort to create a solid bottom. Trains ran over the spot for several years without incident. One morning, however, a train crew was sent to pull in a string of loaded flat cars which had been standing overnight, and all they found was a gaping hole in the ground. The flat-cars, logs, roadbed, and track remain there still, as they were covered over with tons of gravel and new rail, and later with the highway. Solid bottom was at last achieved.

Two little railroads that flourished east of Manistique along the Soo Line, both of which carried passengers to and from junction points, were the Blaney & Southern, and the Lake Michigan & Superior. The former was built by the Mueller Lumber Company and consisted of eight miles of track between Bear Creek (now Blaney Park) and Blaney Junction. Whereas its name fairly described the route of the Blaney & Southern, its neighbor farther east along the Soo Line carried a title in keeping with the grandiose style of the day. The Lake Michigan & Superior's tracks began at Pike Lake, eight miles north of Lake Michigan, and the closest it ever got to Lake Superior was 25 miles.

The stub track leading off the Soo Line, which was the begin-

The map of train routes on the Keweenaw Peninsula, far left, is taken from a 1913 Michigan Railroad Commission map. The eastern peninsula routes, top left, are from the 1897 Michigan Legislative Manual train map. The map above is from the 1889 Michigan Legislative Manual.

ning of the LM & S, still exists. The grade can be followed from that point to the northwest, crossing US-2 just west of East Milakokia Lake Road. There, located on the north side of the highway, once stood the town of Bryan. It consisted of a post office-store, schoolhouse, a dozen houses, two cook camps, an ice house, and a roundhouse. Beyond Bryan, the road's owners, Stack Lumber Company of Escanaba, built to connect with the Manistique Railway at McEwen Junction. In 1910, it took over the tracks of the road between Wilmans and Seney, thus creating a 44-mile line from Pike Lake to a junction with the South Shore. That same year, the LM & S ceased passenger operations—in 1918, it went out of business. A few years later the Stack people built another railroad to the north, four miles farther east along the Soo Line at Corrine. This line never carried passengers, but it was distinctive in that all its track material—including 26 miles of rail, bars, and tie plates—was rented from the Soo Line and returned after some 15 years of use. The little town of Corrine had at one time been an important Soo Line stop, but when it lost its lime kiln and saw mill, Corrine suffered the humiliation of having its depot jacked up and moved two miles east to a new location at Gould City where a band played to celebrate the arrival.

Another railroad that bridged the distance between the Soo Line and the South Shore was the Manistique & Lake Superior (M & LS). In 78 years, it went through four ownership changes, suffered a number of financial setbacks, and earned several uncomplimentary nicknames. Reflecting its sometimes shaky financial and corporate structure more than its roadbed, it was referred to as the "Haywire." At various times through the years, the railroad had ferry service for both freight and passengers to Northport, Ludington, and Frankfort. Passenger service north along its line was quite extensive, with regular runs through Steuben to Shingleton and a daily trip over the 11-mile branch from Scotts to Jenney. A story is told about agent Hiram Hill, located at Scotts, who once withstood the ravages of a flu epidemic, a feat he proudly attributed to a daily diet of huge raw onions. When everyone else in the area was laid low, a doctor and nurse were sent up from Manistique by special train and were greeted on the station platform by Mr. Hill. In his usual manner of speaking forcefully face to face, he bellowed, "Hello, I'm Hiram Herbert Hill." The doctor and nurse fainted dead away.

The Garden Bay Railroad began in 1908 as a logging road of

The train routes below are taken from a 1913 Michigan Railroad Commission map. Those at bottom right are from a 1956 Michigan Railroad Association map, and the Marquette-to-Menominee route, far right, is from the 1881 Michigan Legislative Manual.

the Van's Harbor Lumber Company. It operated as a common carrier from 1914 to 1917 over the 14 miles between Garden Village and the Soo Line at Cooks, running two mixed trains daily. Old timers recall holiday trips in flag-bedecked cars to Manistique and back in day-long celebration. They also tell of a morning when the road's locomotive couldn't be found. Speculation is that the night watchman—the "hostler" to railroaders—was drunk and failed to notice as the steam pressure fell, the air pump failed, and the engine began to roll backwards. The morning train crew found that the locomotive had backed down to the shore line, over a dock, and into 20 feet of water.

The organizers of the Wisconsin & Michigan Railway dreamed of creating a railroad-car ferry system to connect the U.P.'s rich iron and timber lands with the Chicago market, and in 1894 they began construction. After years of struggle, a line from Peshtigo Harbor, Wisconsin to Iron Mountain was completed. It included two branch lines crossing the Menominee River into Wisconsin and providing service to Marinette-Menominee over the Milwaukee's tracks. By 1903 twice-daily round-trip passenger runs were offered from Peshtigo and Norway, later to Iron Mountain, with a Soo Line connection at Faithorn, where a hotel was built to accommodate passengers awaiting the Minneapolis-Soo trains.

An outstanding feature of the Wisconsin & Michigan was the plush resort it built on Miscauno Island in the Menominee River. The railway's patrons were housed in an elegant hotel completed in 1905 with telephones, marble baths, and electric lights. A special train bore distinguished guests from Chicago for the grand opening, and other specials came from Iron Mountain and Marinette-Menominee to bring the total attendance to more than 500 visitors. Despite well-advertised sleeper service from Minneapolis and Chicago, the hotel couldn't attract enough business on a regular basis, however, and soon shut down. A few other railroads also built hotels and resorts to attract passenger service along their lines, but while most have faded into the past along with the railroads, one famous resort still enjoys a thriving business. The Grand Hotel on Mackinac Island was funded by the New York Central and Pennsylvania Railroads, and provided a glamorous destination for wealthy rail travelers from midwest and eastern cities.

The Munising Railway established a passenger connection with the North Western at Little Lake in November, 1897. En route from Munising, passengers could transfer to the South Shore at

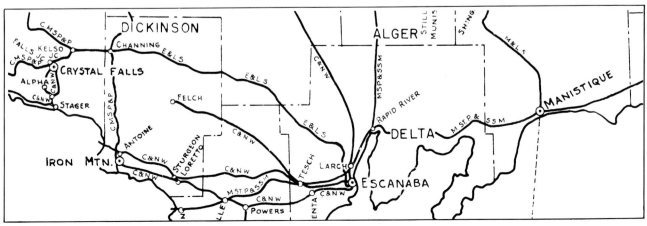

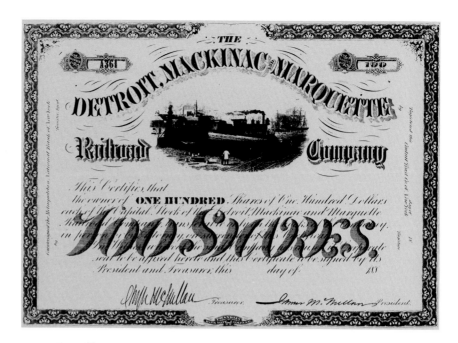

Munising Junction, and east of there its tracks reached Coalwood. By the time the junction was established with its purchaser, the LS & I at Lawson, this small railroad with its 41 miles of track had four trains operating daily in each direction. Like its line, the Munising's corporate life was short, but it's president's business car can still be seen at the Ford Museum in Greenfield Village.

In 1905 the Escanaba & Lake Superior (E & LS) was running twice daily service from Escanaba and Wells to Channing, and two trains on its Northland Branch. Its passenger service was never extensive over the 85 miles. The peak year recorded a passenger count of 16,000, but the revenue per passenger was little more than a dollar. In the last two years of operation, 1955-56, the combined total passenger revenue was $17.22. By surviving today as a freight

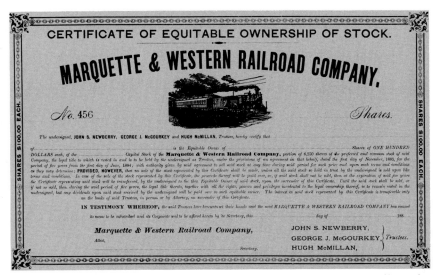

CERTIFICATE OF EQUITABLE OWNERSHIP OF STOCK.

MARQUETTE & WESTERN RAILROAD COMPANY,

No. 456   *Shares.*

The undersigned, JOHN S. NEWBERRY, GEORGE J. McGOURKEY *and* HUGH McMILLAN, *Trustees, hereby certify that*

Marquette & Western Railroad Company,
Attest.

JOHN S. NEWBERRY,
GEORGE J. McGOURKEY, } *Trustees.*
HUGH McMILLAN,

carrier, the E & LS is unique in that it operates 208 more miles of track than it did 80 years ago.

The majority of daily trains were, of course, main-line runs, but service wasn't lacking on the branches of the major roads. Round-trip runs were made on the Soo Line's Rapid River branch to Eben Junction and a connection with the Munising Railway. The Milwaukee, off its Ontonagon branch, had a line running from Kelso to Crystal Falls and later to Iron River. The LS & I built a line north to Big Bay from Marquette. The North Western ran passenger trains on seven branches. Mixed trains were run on the Whitefish branch from Winde, present day Perkins, through Friday, Osier, and Diffin to the sawmill settlement of Ladoga in Alger County. Ten miles west of Escanaba at Narenta, a stretch which was double tracked at one time because of heavy traffic, the Felch Mountain branch canted off to the northwest crossing the Escanaba, Iron Mountain & Western (Schlesinger branch), and the Soo Line at Tesch. Daily service on this line had stops at Alecto, Perronville, Whitney, Dryads, Faunas, Hylas, Foster City, and Metropolitan.

Commonly called the "Ore Line" because it was the route of loaded ore trains from Antoine to Escanaba, the Schlesinger branch boasted a daily mixed train that portrayed the kind of mile-by-mile service on which communities, no matter how small, depended. This train started from Powers in the morning, traveled to Iron Mountain and Antoine, then east down the Schlesinger to Tesch. It rejoined the main line at Narenta and completed the circular trip at Powers. It provided freight and passenger service at 27 stops, many of which were too tiny to be called anything but a "place." West of Iron Mountain, the Crystal Falls branch left the main line at Stager and had three daily trains both ways that ran through to Amasa. At Iron River there was a daily round trip on the branch to Atkinson.

Rarely did the tracks of any U.P. railroad dead end, for like a giant maze, the rails were interconnected at more than 100 points. Except for periodic two- and three-day stops in the larger towns, the ubiquitous traveling salesman with his trunk of samples spent perhaps one-third of his time on trains. His calls put him off at stations and on again hours later, changing at branch-line junctions to travel to the end of the line and back, or to transfer to another railroad. A salesman might cover the entire peninsula by rail on an

These railroad stock certificates were issued in the 1880s when shares were selling for $100 each.

63

photo by Childs Art Gallery, courtesy of Superior View, Marquette

annual trip that could keep him traveling for several weeks.

Passenger equipment varied considerably depending on whether the cars were on through runs or local runs. The day coaches were of all-wood construction, gas lighted, heated with coal stoves that fried the nearest passengers and left those farthest away marginally chilly. They were also equipped with private but crude toilets which afforded a view of the roadbed below. Cinders worked their way inside throughout the seasons, but particularly when the weather was hot and the windows were opened. But with all its discomforts, train travel was far superior to the alternatives.

Pullman sleepers were the first cars to be electrically lighted and steam heated, and the "palace" cars on through runs to the East Coast over the Soo Line and South Shore were outfitted in the opulent style of the day. Regular overnight trains to and from such cities as Minneapolis and Chicago offered standard Pullman service with plush green upholstered seats by day and 12 section upper and lower berths by night. Dining cars were the pride of most railroads, and often the subject of competitive advertising. Snow-white linen, sparkling table service, and excellent cuisine produced meals that were equal to those of the finest big-city dining establishments.

The busiest place in town throughout the day and half the night was the railroad depot. The comings and goings of passengers were enough to keep a depot busy, but in addition, it was also where all the town's mail and much of its merchandise, via the Railway Express Agency, were dispatched. Often it was the sole source of telegraph communication. Most depots had dining rooms and waiting rooms which were well patronized by passengers and their friends, and by the number of men whose work brought them to the station. To keep operations running smoothly required baggage men, an agent, ticket clerk, car inspector, crossing watchman, crewmen changing with those arriving, and perhaps a waiting switch-engine crew to add or remove cars. A streetcar crew could be waiting, plus drivers of rigs, a newsboy or two, and the draymen who took the trunks to and from the depot.

Excursion trains were fun and provided for all sorts of adventures. For example, one September Sunday in 1900, special trains brought an estimated 1,000 people to Escanaba to enjoy the

Trains carried both passengers and freight in and out of the important port city of Marquette.

64

photo from the Frank Bourke Collection

facilities along the bay. The travelers watched a ball game, went swimming and picnicking, took boat rides on the steamer *Lotus*, then boarded the trains in the evening for the return trip home.

Then came the automobile...and a rapid decline in the number of railroad passengers. By the 1920s, trains simply could not compete with the obvious advantages of the car. The Great Depression reduced rail traffic even further, and by 1934 only 34 trains in the U.P. were running daily, and only four of them were in the Copper Country. By then, the Copper Range had no scheduled passenger runs, just mixed trains. World War II caused a sharp, although temporary, increase in rail passengers all over the country, and the few remaining U.P. trains were strained to meet the peak demands. During Christmas weekend of 1942, about 1,100 passengers were carried on two sections of the North Western's *Peninsula 400* into Marinette-Menominee. Three mornings later, 550 people boarded the south-bound run at Escanaba. This was an all-time record for passengers boarded at a single depot north of Green Bay. From then on, however, business plummeted. Train after train was removed from service despite loud protests about their value to the public—a public which wasn't riding them. On July 15, 1969, the *Peninsula 400,* the only remaining passenger train, began its last round trip from Ishpeming to Chicago. Other than a Sunday-only, round trip Chicago-Menominee run which operated until the advent of Amtrak on May 1, 1971, the Upper Peninsula's 105-year history of railroad passenger service had come to an end.

Seventy-five years after the predominance of the passenger train, there is barely a visible reminder of its presence in the entire U.P. Here and there one can find an old and rotting wooden passenger car. And a few depots, once the community hub, still stand, although most have been torn down. There are no circus trains, and you can't go to the depot at night and mail a letter at a railway post office mail car and have it delivered the next morning, 350 miles away. You can't even find the towns of Bryan, Wilman, Ladoga, or Atkinson. But you *can* find the former town of Diffin, where the North Western's Whitefish branch crossed US-41, northwest of Trenary, where the school teacher from Escanaba used to come in every Monday on the mixed train...

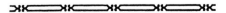

One of the train stops in the southern part of the U.P. was Hermansville, where travelers were greeted by this depot.

photo courtesy of Superior View, Marquette

Crossroads At The Fox River

Seney came with the railroad. The year was 1881. Michigan was building the first rail link connecting its two peninsulas, and crews were busy laying track west from St. Ignace and east from Marquette. Upper Peninsula pioneer Peter White drove the last spike as the rails met just east of Newberry, and the long dreamed Detroit, Mackinac & Marquette Railroad became a reality! Names of the railroad's directors and other prominent persons were given to stations along the route—mostly sidings every half-dozen miles for loading logs and lumber—little more than wide spots in the grade. George L. Seney, a DM & M director from New York, gave his name to milepost 79, where the tracks crossed the Fox River.

Three big lumber companies were already operating in the vast area drained by the Manistique River and its tributaries. As the cut of vast stands of pine moved northward up the Manistique River and its tributaries, a base was needed closer to woods operations. The Fox and its branches was a good river system to drive; a series of dams was built all the way to near its source—within a few miles of Lake Superior. A big territory in northeast Schoolcraft County soon was set up as Seney Township, and late in December of 1882, a post office was established in the "town." Seney was on the map!

It was in a good location as a focal point for the logging business but, as a town site, Seney left something to be desired. In the spring, the Fox frequently flooded its banks, and for most of the rest of the year the water table was just a few feet below the ground. Many of the buildings were elevated on cedar posts, and the board sidewalks were raised well above the grade of the muddy streets. But swamp or no, Seney lost no time becoming a busy logging center. Its streets were soon lined with saloons and hotels—and a handful of dwellings—and the 1884 census listed the population at 180.

Other logging companies extended their operations to the Seney area. General Russell A. Alger of Detroit (who became William McKinley's Secretary of War during the Spanish-American conflict, and later a U.S. Senator) made Seney the headquarters for his Manistique Lumbering Company, which held big tracts of pine north toward Grand Marais. In 1886 Alger established the Manistique Railway at Seney. The railway began with a six-mile stretch of track from Seney north to Hoist, a point on the East Branch of the Fox River where logs were taken out to avoid the swampy "Spreads" a short distance downstream. The railroad eventually pushed its tracks south to Germfask and Curtis, and north all the

At left, the Incredible Seney Museum is located on the "old" main street in what used to be the depot and the town hall.

67

photo courtesy of Michigan State Archives, Lansing

photo from the collection of Jack Riordan

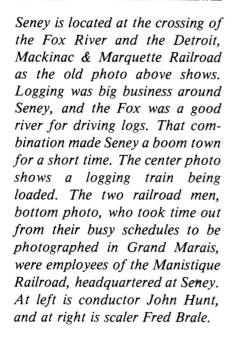

Seney is located at the crossing of the Fox River and the Detroit, Mackinac & Marquette Railroad as the old photo above shows. Logging was big business around Seney, and the Fox was a good river for driving logs. That combination made Seney a boom town for a short time. The center photo shows a logging train being loaded. The two railroad men, bottom photo, who took time out from their busy schedules to be photographed in Grand Marais, were employees of the Manistique Railroad, headquartered at Seney. At left is conductor John Hunt, and at right is scaler Fred Brale.

photo courtesy of Seney Museum

68

way to Grand Marais. Carrying passengers and freight as well as logs, the railroad helped make Seney a busy rail transit point. The DM&M also made it a division headquarters.

There were lumbering towns springing up all over the eastern Upper Peninsula in the 1880s with the building of the DM&M and the Minneapolis, St. Paul & Sault Ste. Marie (Soo Line) railroads. These two roughly parallel lines opened up vast areas of country. Much of it had been granted to the railroads as an inducement to building through the sparsely populated region. Newberry, Trout Lake, Shingleton, and several dozen other hamlets became lumber centers buzzing with activity, but Seney became the most notorious of them all. "Hell Town in the Pine" it came to be called, ranking in notoriety with Tombstone, Deadwood, and other rough towns of the Wild West. Seney was sensationalized in the nation's press; the bawdy houses, saloon fights and murders, the gambling and general lawlessness in this northwoods town became the subject of many a story over the years. There were even reports of a "stockade" of young women kept in the woods near Seney to furnish bordellos back in town, and a rumor that "slave" labor was used in lumber camps. In later years, books were written about Seney and Upper Peninsula pine logging, most of them repeating and sometimes adding to the legends of the area.

With great reluctance, it must be admitted that many of the tales about Seney are only tales—nothing more. That isn't to say Seney didn't have a colorful past. It did. But it apparently was no worse than the dozens of other mining and lumbering towns in the Upper Peninsula. There are those around Seney who had more than a little fun with writers over the years, perpetuating—and sometimes enlarging—the "Hell Town" reputation.

It all began during the winter of 1886 when a noted temperance advocate from Detroit was making a tour of the Upper Peninsula. She wrote to J.B. Wheeler, an agent for the Chicago Lumber Company at Seney, saying she wanted to deliver an address there. Knowing well the benefits that sobriety would bring to the several hundred lumberjacks it had on its payrolls in the area, the company welcomed her visit. One old account said "...the lumbering people entertained her royally. The woods boys dressed up in their best and attended her lecture, maintaining their best deportment." She stayed for several days and was taken to visit some of the camps. Shortly before her departure, however, a few of the jacks who attended her lecture, and some others who had drifted into town during her stay, got drunk "and shook things up quite a bit." To make matters worse, a party of traveling salesmen, observing the antics, wanted to have their share of fun. They got into a lively conversation with the woman, and by the time she was ready to board the train, they had made her believe that "half the town was composed of saloons and that the others were disreputable houses."

On her return to Detroit, the temperance lady was interviewed by several newspaper reporters, and the image of a rip-roaring "hell town" spread across the country. Twenty-five years later, an old lumberjack who was in Seney at the time recalled: "The woman was a thoroughly honest old dame and I never believed that she really intended the harm that came from her visit."

The late William S. Crowe was one of Schoolcraft County's

leading bankers for many years. During the white pine heyday, he was bookkeeper for the Chicago Lumber Company. "I knew all the camp foremen very well and most of the lumberjacks by face and name, and was acquainted with many of them," Crowe writes in his book *Lumberjack*. Calling the portraying of the pine days in recent literature "fantastic and unrealistic," he says that "this generation [has been given] a greatly distorted picture of those times." He concedes that old-timers liked to tell tall tales, especially if the interviewer was getting material for a book, "...in which case they went all out and outdid themselves inventing Bunyanesque tales."

The late John J. (Jack) Riordan, Seney historian and author, agreed that the tales got taller as the years went on. Riordan had worked as a railroad station agent-telegrapher and was a resident of the community for more than 60 years. He arrived shortly after the pine era ended and, compared to the *really* notorious towns across the country, Riordan put it bluntly, "Seney was a virgin!"

Seney continued to grow. In May of 1888, the editor of the *Newberry News* took inventory in Seney: 3 hotels, 11 residences and 13 saloons. By 1890 the official census gave Seney Township a population of 937, which included the hundreds of lumberjacks in the woods. This was the recorded highpoint for the township, although unofficially it may have passed the 1,000 mark in the mid- and late '80s. Buildings continued to sprout up along Pennsylvania Avenue, Railroad Street and Seney Avenue. Lumber was about the cheapest commodity around and local carpenters were kept busy. Some accounts say Seney had 29 saloons; others put the total at 21. Actually, not more than about a dozen were in operation at any one time and, by 1894, the number dwindled to about six. Dan Dunn's saloon was probably the most notorious. Coming to Seney from Roscommon, Dunn soon established a reputation of keeping one step ahead of the sheriff.

In spite of their reputation, Seney folks participated in the usual assortment of wholesome activities such as church socials, picnics, politics, baseball, trout fishing, and the other pastimes which made up life in small town America at the time. One newspaper reporter in the early 1890s went so far as to call Seney "one of the most orderly towns," adding, "The saloons are closed on Sundays and national holidays." But it was the rough side of life there that caught the nation's attention. Two incidents in particular did much to give the town its undeserved image.

The Harcourts carried a lot of weight in Seney—not much went on in town without at least their tacit approval. Most people liked the Harcourt boys: Tom, Luke, Bill, Steve, Dick, and Jim, but saloon keeper Dan Dunn was an exception. Their rivalry reportedly began years earlier when both families lived in Roscommon. It climaxed on June 25, 1891, when Dunn fatally shot 20-year-old Steve who had come into his saloon to buy a friend a drink. Dunn was acquitted on self-defense, and the Harcourts decided to take the law into their own hands. A short time later, Jim Harcourt shot and killed Dunn in a saloon in Trout Lake. Harcourt was sentenced to seven years in the state prison in Marquette, but was released for good behavior after serving three years. The people of Seney had petitioned the governor for his release, and many thought he had "done the town a favor" by ridding it of the notorious Dunn. Har-

photo courtesy of Michigan State Archives, Lansing

photo courtesy of Michigan State Archives, Lansing

photo courtesy of Seney Museum

These photos are old views of Seney. The top photograph was taken looking west on Railroad Street. Children gathered on the steps of their school to be included in the center photo. The Grondin Hotel, bottom, was a popular establishment in Seney. It burned to the ground for the second time in 1919.

photo courtesy of Seney Museum

court returned to be elected township supervisor for nine terms. He later became deputy sheriff and a conservation officer.

The other notorious incident took place on Christmas Eve, 1894, when lumberjack Isaac Stetcher killed Manistique Lumber Company foreman Thomas Kane. The two men had apparently been arguing back at camp and resumed their quarrel later, in Hugh Logan's saloon. Stetcher challenged Kane to finish the fight in the street. Kane's friends restrained him, but as soon as their attention went to something else, he slipped out. In the scuffle which followed, Stetcher stabbed Kane, who died instantly. Stetcher was put in the town jail and the *Marquette Mining Journal* reported, "There were threats of lynching, and it was feared that the building in which he [Stetcher] was confined might be fired during the night, so a heavy guard was placed about it." Stetcher was sentenced to a seven-year term in the Marquette prison.

A few of the local jacks have also contributed to the legend which has grown up around Seney. P.K. Small, an educated man from the East who seldom spoke of his past, was reportedly a panhandler and prankster. He is said to have bitten off heads of snakes and birds to win drinks in a saloon, and shook loose change out of pockets of passengers as they detrained at the depot. Author Crowe, however, remembers a different sort of fellow. "I knew P.K. Small very well," he wrote. "I never saw or heard of him biting the heads off snakes, birds or toads for a drink, nor that some other lumberjack bit P.K.'s nose off because P.K. had bitten the head off the other fellow's pet owl, until I read these tales in a book written by an author who wasn't born until four years after the last of the big pine had been cut."

"Silver Jack" Driscoll was another of Seney's infamous residents for a while. He came to town to tend bar for his former Roscommon friend, Dan Dunn, and later worked in camps around Seney. As a fighter, Silver Jack was feared and respected throughout Michigan's North Country. Fighting was probably the thing the jacks and other local characters actually did most often, a fact which contributed to the reputation of Seney. Some, of course, were real knock-down, drag-out battles, but fighting for the fun of it provided a lot of good entertainment.

These lovely ladies were known as the Seney Belles. They are from left: Sadie McLeod, Easter Harcourt, Misey McLeod, Sarah Grace, and Florence McLeod.

photo courtesy of Seney Museum

In the 1890s, logging activity began to shift north and Seney started on a downhill slide. The town's biggest setback came with extension of the Manistique Railway from Beaver Junction 10 miles north to Grand Marais in 1893. The Manistique Lumbering Company began shipping all its logs by rail to a newly rebuilt mill at Grand Marais. Within a short time, the railroad moved its office, roundhouse and shops from Seney to Grand Marais, and the exodus to the "promising new town on Lake Superior" started. Several of the town's proprietors caught what was dubbed the "Grand Marais disease" and headed north. Whole shops and houses were knocked down in sections, loaded on flatcars, and rebuilt in Grand Marais. By 1900, Seney was reduced to about half its peak population of the 1880s. But it remained a busy rail junction and transit point. Devastation came to the entire area around 1910 when the pine played out and the loggers moved on to other locations, mainly to the West Coast. In 1909, the big pine mill closed in Grand Marais and in 1910 the Manistique Railway was abandoned. Grand Marais became almost a ghost town, and Seney's population dwindled to just over 100. The "pine plains" north of Seney stretched for miles, a burned-over wasteland of charred stumps. There were big stands of hardwood near Germfask, Curtis and Grand Marais, but cutting had not begun to any large extent. There didn't seem to be much of a future for Seney.

Just as the glory days seemed gone forever, hope was rekindled. In 1911, more than 250,000 acres of land in the Seney and Tahquamenon swamps were bought by a Saint Paul, Minnesota company for—of all things—agricultural development! The Western Land Securities Company was said to have purchased more than 700,000 acres of swamplands in Schoolcraft, Chippewa, Luce and Mackinac counties. H.H. Hamilton, president of the firm, announced in January, 1911, that the purchase "means opening up and placing upon the market thousands of acres of farming lands upon terms that will invite rapid settlement and cultivation."

The company soon began what was called the largest private drainage effort ever undertaken in Michigan. Two parallel ditches were planned west of Seney, to be about five miles apart, draining into the Manistique River. A big gasoline dredge was soon at work

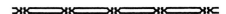

Written across the face of this photograph is "Grand Marais-Seney Stage." Notice the suitcases leaning against the engine cover.

73

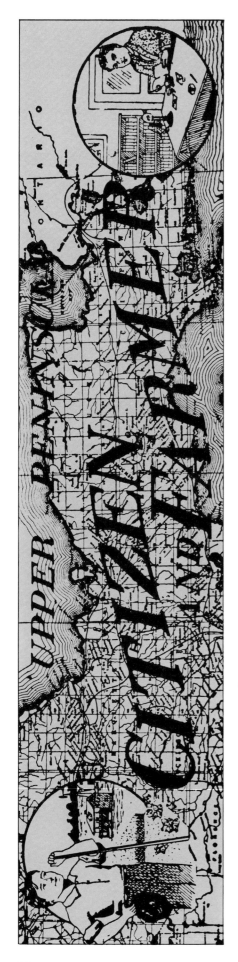

photo courtesy of Michigan State Archives, Lansing

in the swamp, and before the whole idea fell apart, many miles of the 20-foot ditches were actually dug. The company sent A.K. Gordon to Seney as its general agent, and a "New Seney" town site was laid out on higher ground just west of the old village. Shops, office buildings and two imposing homes were built, and prospective investors and settlers began to visit New Seney. Hamilton predicted, "The present year will witness the greatest influx of homeseekers into Northern Michigan ever known."

A few families did arrive, and by early 1912 the Western Land Securities Company claimed to have "sold all [our] land holdings for ten miles out of New Seney." What one contemporary newspaper account called "the Great Dismal Swamp" was being drained and turned into an agricultural cornucopia—or so it seemed. A group of hopeful Belgians began to develop farms about five miles northwest of town, a settlement referred to as "Belgiquia." The project gained much attention in the Midwest and was widely advertised and promoted by Western Land Securities. It attracted several substantial investors who established prosperous farms that produced livestock, hay, oats, rye, and wheat.

So what finally went wrong? Fires, of course, destroyed much potentially productive soil. Joseph A. Jeffery, agricultural agent for the DSS&A, who experimented with soils at Seney, later observed, "Fires...were permitted to burn unhindered, resulting in destruction of soil that appears appalling." Hopes were too high, money ran out, and some of the land was obviously worthless for agriculture. Eventually the bank and most other businesses in New Seney closed doors; the *Citizen and Farmer,* which had begun publishing in 1912, published its last issue in the summer of 1916.

Agent Jeffery had conducted scientific experiments on other Midwestern muck-type soils, and began similar efforts at Seney in the spring of 1918. In an article published in 1925, he reported that "on the Seney swamp soils it has been demonstrated that of the grains, oats, rye, and barley can be successfully grown. Potatoes, rutabagas, turnips, carrots and parsnips do well. Timothy and Alsyk-clover thrive. Strawberries have done finely." The soil seemed to produce well when given liberal amounts of manure and potash, then rolled with a heavy roller at least once a year. Jeffery's experimental plots produced well, and at the Schoolcraft County Fair in 1924, Seney Swamp oats, potatoes, carrots, parsnips and barley took first prizes! But Jeffery moved on, and a lack of interest coupled with continued ravages by fire spelled the end of Seney's days as the "agricultural Mecca" of the North.

Jack Riordan could remember when there were four freight and four passenger trains, and as many as 10 "extras" daily passing through Seney, but times have changed. And so has Seney. When highway M-28 was relocated north on the street paralleling the "old" main street, Seney's business district moved with it. Across the railroad tracks on the "old" main street sits the town hall; next door is the former railroad depot, now restored. The depot and town hall make up the "Incredible Seney Museum." Big logging wheels stand off to one side as reminders of the days when Seney was one of the most notorious lumber towns in the United States.

More than 90,000 acres on the south side of highway M-28, that runs between Shingleton and Seney, have been preserved as the Seney National Wildlife Refuge. Tourism, hunters and anglers, and a few logging operations now provide much of the livelihood for residents of this personable, well-known crossroads. Mennonites have settled in the area throughout the past 30 years; they've built a church and are active in the community. Seney's population stands at about 200—its average for most of this century.

One more recollection was shared by Jack Riordan as his thoughts went back to 1919. The summer was wearing on and blueberries were ripening out on the plains north of town. People by the dozens were going out there, some pitching tents, to pick berries for the major Midwest markets. It had been a good summer, quiet and pleasant. The only excitement around town that year was when Phil Grondin's hotel burned down for the second time. It had been a spectacular blaze which everyone went to see. The town was also welcoming the boys back from the World War. Many were getting mustered out of the army that summer. Riordan was telegrapher at the depot then. He'd arrived in 1916, and was working under Station Agent P.M. Stillman. Just before noon one day in August the westbound passenger train pulled in, and a young man with a pack stepped out on the platform. He had fishing equipment in one hand. His gaze fell on Riordan who was out on the platform helping with the mail and baggage.

"Say, can you tell me where there's a good trout stream around here?" the young man asked Jack, who was about his same age.

"Tell you what," Jack replied. "I'll be going home to lunch in a few minutes. C'mon along with me and I'll show you." The two fell in together for the short walk a few blocks west along Railroad Street toward Jack's house. When they had passed the Fox River bridge, Jack pointed to the abandoned Manistique Railway grade.

"You take that grade north about four miles and you'll hit the East Branch of the Fox—best trout stream around here."

The stranger thanked Jack and shifted his pack to a more comfortable position, eying the grade ahead.

"Good luck," Jack said. "By the way, my name's Jack Riordan." "I'm Ernest Hemingway," the fisherman said. They waved as Hemingway disappeared down the grade to the East Branch for a fishing trip the world will never forget.

TWO LIVE NEW TOWNS IN THE UPPER PENINSULA OF MICHIGAN

New Seney
Located in Schoolcraft County, on D. S. S. & A. R. R.

Trout Lake
In Chippewa County, at the Junction of the Soo Line and the D. S. S. & A, R. R.

TOWNSITES OWNED BY
The WESTERN LAND SECURITIES CO.
HOME OFFICE: ST. PAUL

GORDON, General Townsite Agent
New Seney, Michigan

The Western Land Securities Company began dredging the marsh at Seney, above left, around 1911, and planned to develop "New Seney" as farm land. The Upper Peninsula Citizen and Farmer *logo is from a newspaper that was published in "New Seney" for about four years while the Western Land Securities Company was promoting the area to investors. Even the little booklet above advertising "Two Live New Towns" could not save the "New Seney" project. Eventually the bank and most of the businesses closed their doors, and the newspaper published its last issue in 1916.*

photo courtesy of Marquette County Historical Society

Henry Ford's Upper Peninsula

Sometimes the slim elderly gentleman arrived at the Upper Peninsula by yacht. At other times, a sleek chauffeured limousine brought him and, on occasion, he swooped from the skies in an airplane. But regardless of the way he came, Henry Ford was enthusiastically welcomed by employees, band music, delighted school children, and facilities that gleamed with fresh paint like rejuvenated toys. The automobile king made a tremendous impact on northern Michigan for more than three decades. Ford's vast interests reached from Alger County in the east to Gogebic County in the west, and included sawmill towns, logging camps, iron ore mines, millions of acres of timberland, and much more.

To achieve complete independence in his downstate car factories, Ford believed he should control the sources of needed raw materials. The U.P. was amply blessed in timber and minerals so in 1919, the motor monarch did some scouting around and announced that he intended to buy large tracts of U.P. timberland. Gossip pinned the amount to one million acres. Speculation began immediately, and residents in every village hoped they would benefit from some Ford enterprise. In 1920, Iron Mountain was the first town to be smiled on, but others soon followed. Like a boy in a candy store with a fist filled with coins, Henry Ford went on a buying spree.

Edward Kingsford, who married Ford's cousin, Minnie Flaherty, had a Model-T dealership in Iron Mountain. The former timber cruiser, acting as Ford's agent, purchased the holdings of the Michigan Iron and Land Company which included almost a million acres of land. In addition, early in 1921, Kingsford bought the 160-acre Joseph Mongrain farm on the city's outskirts for a proposed factory site. (It was incorporated as the village of Kingsford in 1923.) Land values rose drastically. One of the world's most modern sawmills was the first unit built. On July 12, the first huge log was ripped into boards, and by November, the mill began shipping lumber downstate for use in Model-Ts.

Before long, the complex included three body plants which fashioned Model-T floorboards and frames, numerous dry kilns, a chemical plant, and a refinery. The chemical plant produced charcoal briquets, and became one of Henry's more profitable businesses. About 100 tons were made daily year-round. Methanol, an antifreeze solution; ethyl acetate, a paint solvent; and several other substances were manufactured there as well.

To power his plants, Ford constructed a hydraulic dam on the

Henry Ford's camp at the Huron Mountain Club, pictured at left, was built in 1930 from huge hand-hewn logs. Ford waited seven years to be accepted for membership in the exclusive club.

Menominee River. It is one of his few original enterprises still operating, now owned by the Wisconsin-Michigan Power Company. Within walking distance of the dam is a bustling airport. Ford deeded the field to Dickinson County in the 1930s, specifying that it always be used as an airport, and that it retain the Ford name.

By 1927, there was a decline in the use of wooden parts with the coming of the Model-A and V-8. Station wagon bodies began to be made at the Kingsford/Iron Mountain facility, and by 1939, their production was in full swing. Stake and flat-bed truck bodies were fashioned there as well. When World War II started, the entire plant joined in the war effort by manufacturing Waco CG4A gliders (C for combat, G, glider,) with 4,500 persons working three shifts, 24 hours a day. After the procedure was perfected eight gliders were turned out daily. During a three-year period, the company made 4,190 units, each formed from more than 70,000 parts.

On D-day when the skies of France were filled with warring aircraft, Kingsford/Iron Mountain gliders were part of a fifty-mile caravan silently carrying men and supplies behind enemy lines. The gliders received the coveted Army-Navy "E" award for their excellent performance. While there has been disagreement about their efficiency, John Huska of the WWII Glider Pilots Association remembers, "I piloted one and they were the best."

In the early 1920s, Ford had his eye on the towns of L'Anse and Pequaming, located on Lake Superior's shores. He acquired the L'Anse sawmill from the Sterns and Culver Lumber Company, and bought the entire town of Pequaming from the Hebard Lumber Company. The sale included approximately 400,000 acres of land. In addition, he purchased railroad docks, a fleet of barges and tugs, three locomotives and some railroad to transport logs and lumber to and from these mills. Soon, he had blazed a railroad through the forest from L'Anse to Pequaming to facilitate these operations, and to complement the Lake Superior water route.

During the next few years, Ford perfected these possessions. Pequaming, his pet project, was turned into a model village to test

The Waco CG4A gliders were manufactured at Ford's Kingsford/Iron Mountain plant for use during World War II. After the assembly procedure, which involved more than 70,000 pieces, was perfected, eight gliders could be turned out daily.

photo courtesy of Marquette County Historical Society

his theories on self-reliance and education. Hebard had built the once-attractive homes and businesses, but Ford completely remodeled them. The old mills were re-bricked; deteriorated buildings were covered with cedar shingles to match the new buildings; and electricity, running water, and indoor toilets were installed. Gallons of paint added gleam to the model community, which in future years received a complete redoing whenever Ford visited there. The wife of a former employee remembered, "When the steam pipes in the plant needed repairs it was discovered that almost an inch of paint covered the insulation."

Besides renovating, Ford erected elementary schools, a high school, and a vocational shop where boys were taught factory skills, and girls learned homemaking arts. In every schoolroom, old-fashioned dancing was a requisite.

A short way from the employees' homes, Hebard had constructed a large bungalow patterned after southern mansions and furnished exquisitely. It became a Ford summer cottage.

Louis DeLongchamp of Negaunee, my uncle, started working in Pequaming in 1924, and remained for nine years. "Everyone was required to take a physical which cost $5.00," he said. "I passed, and as a tractor operator my duties included keeping the mill clean, hauling sawdust, slabs, and garbage, and grading the roads."

Men were paid $5.00 for an eight-hour day for the first three months. If they proved themselves, they became permanent employees and were given a dollar per day raise to boot. Every worker was required to punch a time clock.

DeLongchamp remembers Ford's partiality to paint and cleanliness, and his soft spot for children. "When he planned a visit the mill shut down and everybody painted," he recalled. "Even the carriage used to carry logs was stained and varnished just as the floors were. Once when he came, kids gathered outside of the bungalow gate waiting. He had the chauffeur stop, he got out, and asked them what they wanted. The next day I was grading ground for their skating rink, an area was fenced off, and a change house went up.

Ford bought the town of Big Bay in the 1940s, and resumed operations at the previously idle Big Bay Mill in 1944.

photo courtesy of Marquette County Historical Society

79

photo courtesy of L'Anse Township Hall

photo courtesy of Marquette County Historical Society

Unlike the old-time logging accommodations, Ford's model work camps featured electric lights, running water and central heating. The top photo shows the Ford Motor Company Camp 4 which was located near Watton. Ford's purchase of the town of Big Bay included the Big Bay Hotel, center. After it was renovated, it became a fancy showplace with several sleeping rooms, attractive lounging facilities, a public dining room, and Ford's private quarters. The production of station wagon bodies was in full swing by 1939 at the Kingsford/Iron Mountain facility, bottom photo.

photo courtesy of Menominee Range Museum, Iron Mountain

From then on, one man's chore was keeping the rink in shape."

On another occasion in preparation for a Ford inspection, cantaloupe-sized rocks which lined the trail to the office were painted white. But this didn't bring the expected praise. "Instead when he spotted them he told us to pick them up," DeLongchamp explained. "Claimed they reminded him of a cemetery!"

Ford forbade his employees to keep cows and chickens because he thought they were unsanitary. He believed that on the wages he paid they could afford to buy milk and eggs from his company store. "There was just about anything you could think of in that place," DeLongchamp remembers. "Prices were low. We wore badges which sported a Model-T radiator for identification and to keep out non-employees trying to take advantage of the bargains."

Logs used in the construction of Ford's cabin at the exclusive Huron Mountain Club were cut from behind Pequaming and hand hewn by a few broadax men in 1930. His bungalow became one of the most impressive on club property although he was initially refused membership, and waited seven years for acceptance.

When the Depression hit, Ford was one of the U.P.'s major landholders and employers. More than 10,000 men received greater than $1 million monthly in wages, giving the depressed mining and logging industries an important shot in the arm. Pequaming boomed until downstate auto sales lagged. All of Ford's mills continued running, although on a limited basis. Ford provided each family with a garden plot, and sent many of the men, who otherwise would have been laid off, to clear a section of land on the Skanee Road near L'Anse for $3.00 a day.

"Rumors made the rounds that Ford intended to put in soybeans. But after we harvested the timber, burned the brush, and plowed the huge field, it never was planted," DeLongchamp stated. "Later, it was rented out and is now covered with Christmas trees."

In addition to his sawmills, the Tin Lizzy tycoon's plan of independence for his auto plants included having his own lumber camps to supply his mills with logs. The first of several was built near Sidnaw. He designed a model lumber camp setup just as he had his model sawmill village at Pequaming. Unlike the usual stark shacks with frugal furnishings, his bunkhouses and living quarters had indoor toilets, electricity, central heating, showers, and painted walls. Cement sidewalks connected each building. Tin plates and cups were replaced by china, and filled with delicious, varied food. Weekly laundry service was also available. Wood workers adjusted quickly to these amazing comforts deep in the wilderness. However, such fancy frills, and perhaps a tinge of jealousy, prompted other jacks to nickname Ford's employees "lumber ladies." His woodcutters, like mill workers, were paid $6.00 for each eight-hour day.

The harvested logs were shipped from Sidnaw to Iron Mountain/Kingsford (about 65 miles) by rail. Other Ford camps were set-up in much the same way. Upkeep of these modern quarters was expensive. Then, too, Ford insisted that his lumberjacks practice selective cutting, harvesting mature trees while leaving the younger ones. He also demanded that brush be burned so unwanted fires would be less likely to start. These measures added to production costs so his logging operations were phased out when he discovered he could buy logs more cheaply than he could produce them.

photo courtesy of the Ford Archives, Dearborn

Pictured above is the man who brought great prosperity to the Upper Peninsula—Henry Ford.

photo by Childs Art Gallery, courtesy of Superior View, Marquette

When Ford acquired large land tracts in 1921, he bought the Imperial Mine near Michigamme as well. It had been closed for eight years, but was reopened, and began yielding ore. However, it was of inferior quality. The Blueberry mine began operating in 1929, even though the shaft site and adjoining property six miles west of Ishpeming had been purchased several years earlier. Exeor "Dukes" St. Onge of Ishpeming was a foreman in the Kingsford chemical plant, and later worked in both mines. St. Onge recalls how the Blueberry was christened. Ford and his son, Edsel, came during the early stages of construction to check the progress.

"They walked to the west behind the garage," explained St. Onge. "Old Henry stooped and picked a handful of big blueberries. Suddenly he turned to Edsel and said, 'I'm going to name this mine the Blueberry.' "

Unlike other area mines, the Blueberry was kept exceptionally clean. It had a heated underground lunchroom which was painted every six months. Even the pump house deep in the earth's bowels was redone several times each year.

"To my knowledge it also was the only underground facility in the world with a sidewalk in the main drift," St. Onge said. "One worker did nothing but sweep it clean."

According to St. Onge, who met and chatted with Ford on different occasions, "He was a fair man, put on no airs, and listened intently to anything we had to say." One day St. Onge, who was supposed to be underground, surfaced. He sat on a bench petting a dog, another taboo because animals weren't supposed to enter the buildings. Ford dropped in unexpectedly. "He plunked down beside me and gabbed for a half hour or so helping me pet the dog," St. Onge admitted. "He didn't mention a thing, but I sure got that pooch out in a hurry when he left."

The Imperial and Blueberry Mines were closed in 1933. The Imperial never reopened, but the Blueberry, which was sold to the North Range Mining company, produced ore until 1954.

Ford's self-sustaining Alberta mill began operating in 1938, though the idea was conceived as early as 1935. Alberta, named for a brother-in-law's daughter, lies ten miles south of L'Anse. Forty acres were cleared originally. A sawmill, schools, and a dozen houses were built. Across from them, Ford Lake, now open to the public, was created by damming a creek. The mill, like Ford's

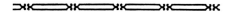

On July 11, 1925, Ford's Imperial Mine employees held a "Safety First" rally in Michigamme.

82

others, was spruced up with a varnished interior, hardwood floors, and well-oiled machinery which hummed in a dirt-free environment. Manpower shortages during WWII forced the mill to close, but it reopened soon after the war. In 1954, the Ford Motor Company bequeathed Alberta to Michigan Technological University at Houghton for use as a forestry research center. In addition to the sawmill and other buildings, 1,703 acres of adjacent timberlands were donated. Since then, additional forest land has been acquired bringing the total to more than 4,000 acres. The original structures are intact and in shipshape condition. Alberta has become the pride of MTU, and has gained worldwide recognition.

photo courtesy of Ford Archives, Dearborn

While summering at the Huron Mountain Club in the early 1940s, Ford bought the town of Big Bay. In addition to an idle sawmill and its machinery, he obtained numerous homes, a general store, a hotel, and other buildings which he reportedly window-dressed to the tune of millions. Operations at the mill resumed in 1944. The output was mainly sent to L'Anse and Iron Mountain with the remainder going to Ford's main plant at River Rouge.

The redecorated hotel became a showplace equal to any major city's fanciest inn. Its lobby boasted a dramatic fireplace with an abundance of space, and attractive lounging facilities. A public dining room accommodated 65 persons. The private Ford dining room was adjacent to the main dining hall. Also, housed on the first floor was the post office, a dentist's office, and a barber shop. Numerous sleeping rooms lined the upstairs, including the Ford suite. Ford was in his golden years when Big Bay was bought, but he took a keen interest in all that went on. After the renovation, he visited frequently, coming from his Huron Mountain lodge. He mingled and chatted with young and old alike.

The last addition in his long battery of mills was at Munising in 1944. This, too, overlooked Lake Superior from a scenic spot. The auto magnate went there intending to buy a large motor, but became enthralled with the beautiful harbor and mill setup. When he left, he was the proud owner of the mill as well as the motor. The property was remodeled, and new machinery shipped in, but the mill never did produce any lumber.

Pequaming's mill shut down in 1942, the beginning of the end for the once-bustling community. It has become a ghost town rarely visited since it is off the beaten tourist path. The high water tank with the fancy Ford signature in black is a beacon for boats cruising in nearby Lake Superior waters.

After Henry Ford's retirement in 1945, and his death two years later, his grandson and namesake sold many of the company's U.P. undertakings which were seen to be no longer needed. In 1951, for example, the Kingsford/Iron Mountain plant was sold to the Kingsford Chemical Company. That same year Big Bay's sawmill was silenced. The L'Anse mill closed in 1954, and Alberta passed on to MTU. Huge tracts of Ford timber holdings were eventually sold, but most of the mineral rights were retained. Ford was a sentimentalist who invested millions in the Upper Peninsula. His dreams fired the imaginations and filled the pockets of its natives. Though the financial benefits are gone, Henry Ford's impact is imprinted in minds and hearts. Said St. Onge, nodding his head emphatically, "He was one of the best friends the U.P. ever had."

Pictured above is Henry Ford's purchasing agent, and relative by marriage, Edward Kingsford.

CLOVER-LAND MAGAZINE

Christmas, 1916

DULUTH

SUPERIOR

GOGEBIC

ONTONAGON

HOUGHTON

KEWEENAW

BARAGA

IRON

MARQUETTE

DICKINSON

ALGER

SCHOOLCRAFT

LUCE

CHIPPEWA

MACKINAC

MENOMINEE

DELTA

MINNEAPOLIS ST. PAUL

MILWAUKEE

DUBUQUE

CHICAGO

BURLINGTON

PEORIA

SPRINGFIELD

Seven Million Fertile Acres in the Upper Peninsula of Michigan

reprinted from Cloverland magazine

Cloverland, My Cloverland

Adventurers, hucksters, politicians, and romantics who have roamed the Upper Peninsula's dense forests, trod its trails, climbed its peaks, and plied its waters have tried for centuries to christen the peninsula with a name that would portray all its facets. While most of the nicknames fell quickly by the wayside, poetic and heavily promoted *Cloverland* lingered for years. There was a *Cloverland* magazine, Cloverland Dairy, Clover-Land candy, a song called Cloverland, and the Cloverland Trail stretching from Ironwood to Sault Ste. Marie. John Bellaire of Schoolcraft County called his farm Clover-Meadow. Leo Patrick Cook wrote lyrics for "My Clover-Land Gal." The Upper Peninsula Development Bureau published a map of Cloverland, a history of Cloverland, and a brochure of where to fish in Cloverland.

Colonel Charles Mott is usually credited with coining the well publicized nickname, but the fervor really began when Roger Andrews moved to Menominee in 1901 to become the editor of the *Menominee Herald Leader.* Andrews arrived in the Upper Peninsula at the beginning of the transition period between the last of the white pine and whatever lay ahead. Much of the land stood neglected in the aftermath of ax and saw, with stumps stretching for miles. In the southern part of the peninsula, however, farmers had discovered rich soil where the hardwoods had grown, so they began to dynamite stumps and plant sugar beets. Six days before the first barrel of beet sugar rolled down the ramp at the brand new $850,000 refinery at Menominee, Andrews' first issue of the *Sugar Beet News* rolled off the presses. The monthly journal, which sold for 50 cents a year, contained a bold, optimistic sort of journalism which was to characterize Andrews' publications for a quarter of a century. "Beet sugar factories are springing up on every side," he wrote. But, in truth, the Menominee River Sugar Company was the only beet sugar factory in the Upper Peninsula. The *Sugar Beet News* reflected other aspects of life in the year 1903. Early issues carried ads for kerosene oil at 12 cents a gallon, Dr. Freel's Cough Balsam, horse blankets for $1.25, good fur robes for $4.50, and men's fleece-lined underwear for 39 cents a suit.

In 1904, Andrews began publishing the *Northwestern Farmer,* which later became *Cloverland.* He presented the Upper Peninsula as an agricultural paradise surrounded by hungry markets, and praised it as a drought-free area where farmers plowed in January, and where the fertility of the soil insured bumper crops every year.

Cloverland *magazine promised that green pastures, pure water, healthy livestock, and cheap land could all be found in the Upper Peninsula. This is the cover from the 1916 Christmas issue.*

reprinted from Cloverland magazine

THE ONLY ILLUSTRATED MONTHLY MAGAZINE IN THE UPPER PENINSULA

CLOVER-LAND

"THE GARDEN SPOT OF MICHIGAN"

VOL. I. No. 1   MENOMINEE, MICHIGAN, JANUARY, 1916   50 CENTS A YEAR

There is Room in Old Glory For Another Star

Andrews says:

I am not the leader of any chosen people, nor the arch prophet of the Upper Peninsula.

I am not a candidate for any political office of any sort.

I want to work in the ranks of the loyal company who believe in Clover-Land, who love it and want the world to know it as it is.

I see in this campaign for separate statehood a great opportunity to call the attention of the country to our rich and growing section, endowed in a score of ways beyond many of the older states of the Union.

reprinted from Cloverland magazine

The fervor over Cloverland began when Roger Andrews moved to Menominee in 1901 to become editor of the Menominee Herald Leader. *In 1904, he began publishing the* Northwestern Farmer *which later became* Cloverland. *This first issue cover quotes Andrews in his campaign to make the Upper Peninsula a separate state.*

"The snowy season is a little longer and the snows are a little deeper than other places farther south," he wrote, "but the air is pure, dry, and vitalizing." Truer words were never spoken.

As tall timber fell beneath the saw, and stump vistas opened on every side, many sawmills and timber-related industries moved south. In November of 1910, for example, the Alger-Smith Lumber Company closed down in Grand Marais, spelling disaster to the town of 3,000. Telephone lines were pulled out, and the passenger and freight train which had operated daily for 15 years between Grand Marais and Seney had no further reason to make the run, so it quit. Those who were left behind to starve hoped that commercial fishing would become the local financial backbone, but the population of Grand Marais dropped to 650 within two years while other U.P. cities and communities looked on in despair, fearing the same fate. Ever the optimist, Andrews called together Upper Peninsula business people and promoters and formed the Upper Peninsula Development Bureau, forerunner of today's U.P. Travel and Recreation Association, on February 21, 1911. The following year, the magic word "Cloverland" appeared for the first time.

An Ideal Combination for a Clover-Land Saw Mill

Prescott Standard Band Mill

Made in Menominee

Heavy Service Prescott Verticle Resaw

The Prescott Company

Menominee, Michigan

reprinted from Cloverland magazine

Andrews told everyone who'd listen that clover grew wherever the sun was allowed to peek through the trees—in fence corners, along roads, and "now it springs up by the wayside." He promoted 15 million acres of Upper Peninsula land for cattle grazing. He said no lazy man need apply, but promised that the hustler had a chance to earn a fully-equipped Cloverland farm. "If you believe in favorable climate, pure water, and lots of clover as essentials for economic livestock production," he wrote, "see Cloverland first."

According to Andrews, while the peninsula undoubtedly had some areas which were too sandy or wet to develop, 65 percent of the land was good for agriculture. The Development Bureau, which backed Andrews' ideas, was financed by county boards, landowners, manufacturers and bankers, and it offered cheap land to farmers and ranchers throughout the West. Some 120,000 Upper Peninsula acres were offered with the following terms: No charge for the first two years, herdsmen would pay local taxes for the third and fourth years, and in the fifth year they would pay taxes plus six percent interest on an option to purchase the property. At the end of the fifth year, 10 percent of the purchase price was required, and

Everyone jumped on the Cloverland bandwagon. This ad for a sawmill appeared in Cloverland *magazine in June, 1916.*

terms would be set for future payment at 6 percent interest. Land was selling for $7.50 to $15 an acre. Western sheep raisers came looking for pasture lands because new legislation was then hampering their operations, and they were plagued with droughts and worry as homesteaders crowded in on their few watering holes.

Andrews saw his role as proclaiming the Cloverland story nationwide through his magazine, while others handled land transactions. "I have no ambition to be an industrial Moses, nor a political boss," he said. "I am not a leader of any chosen people, nor an arch prophet of the Upper Peninsula. I have no corner on knowledge or ability, nor do I hope to carry the Upper Peninsula on my shoulders as Atlas was supposed to carry the world." He concluded, "No matter where the first Garden of Eden was located, the present one is in the Upper Peninsula."

Acting on behalf of the Development Bureau, promoter Charles Hutcheson toured the West, promoting Cloverland from ranch to ranch. He returned with Frank Hagenbarth of Salt Lake City, who was then president of the National Wool Growers Association. After a stay in Cloverland, Hagenbarth said he would soon place 20,000 sheep on Upper Peninsula grazing lands. Speaking on the virtues of Cloverland, Hagenbarth related the tale of the Texan who boasted that all Texas needed to make it a paradise was a little better class of people and a bit more moisture. A neighbor reminded him that Hell needed only that.

"I do not put Michigan in the Texas class in that regard," Hagenbarth said. "But I do say that the prime necessity in the Upper Peninsula is more people and less brush and wood."

John Corson and Alexander McGregor of Wyoming bought 800 acres of cutover land west of Newberry, and hired a company to clear the land for the sheep that were expected the following spring. J.L. Gray of Idaho agreed to take 20,000 acres in Marquette County where he planned to graze 15,000 sheep. His trainload arrived in June of 1918 and included forty Union Pacific double-decked sheep cars carrying 12,000 sheep, one carload of horses, and one of equipment. It created quite a stir at Escanaba as hundreds of people showed up to watch. Sheep raisers from Idaho, Colorado, Utah, Wyoming, and Texas moved in behind Gray. Francis R.K. Hewlett of South Dakota took over the Emblagaard Farm at Ives Lake near Big Bay where he planned to graze up to 50,000 sheep.

The song *Cloverland* was heard throughout the peninsula. When it was published in the Upper Peninsula Development Bureau songbook it carried the admonition, "If you want to sing, but think you can't—holler. Nine times out of ten, the fellow next to you is doing the same thing." Number 38 in the book was as follows:

> "Cloverland, Cloverland, she's the
> Whole land of Northern Michigan;
> We love her rocks and rills,
> Her woods and hills,
> Her forests and her lakes so grand.
> She's a bear, she's a bear, we declare
> She is fair beyond compare;
> In going over this land of clover
> We are glad to live in Clover, Cloverland."

At the same time Andrews was promoting sheep for

Menominee County, the Garden Spot of Michigan

"The Gate-Way to Clover-Land"

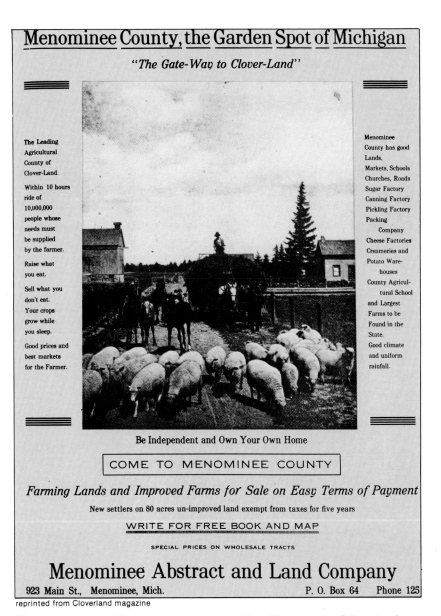

The Leading Agricultural County of Clover-Land.

Within 10 hours ride of 10,000,000 people whose needs must be supplied by the farmer.

Raise what you eat.

Sell what you don't eat. Your crops grow while you sleep.

Good prices and best markets for the Farmer.

Menominee County has good Lands, Markets, Schools Churches, Roads Sugar Factory Canning Factory Pickling Factory Packing Company Cheese Factories Creameries and Potato Ware- houses County Agricul- tural School and Largest Farms to be Found in the State. Good climate and uniform rainfall.

Be Independent and Own Your Own Home

COME TO MENOMINEE COUNTY

Farming Lands and Improved Farms for Sale on Easy Terms of Payment

New settlers on 80 acres un-improved land exempt from taxes for five years

WRITE FOR FREE BOOK AND MAP

SPECIAL PRICES ON WHOLESALE TRACTS

Menominee Abstract and Land Company

923 Main St., Menominee, Mich.   P. O. Box 64   Phone 125

reprinted from Cloverland magazine

Cloverland, the Western Land Securities Company of St. Paul ac- quired a large tract of land in Seney, along the Fox River, and along the Duluth, South Shore & Atlantic Railway. Most of the land was burned-over swampy muskeg, or cutover sandy pine plains. Old- timers said it was so poor you couldn't raise a disturbance on it. However, the company promoted the land as an agricultural paradise. They bought a huge self-propelled gasoline dredge with 12-foot-wide "cat" treads and prepared to ditch and drain the Seney Swamp. Another Minnesota firm showed up with plans to develop the town. They laid out streets for "New Seney," con- structed several pretentious homes, a hotel, bank, general store, drugstore, and newspaper office. In about three years, the Western Land Securities Company had drained enough of the swampland to attract a few farmers. However, they had little luck growing anything on the three-foot-deep muck. One sheep farmer survived until the financial crash of 1929. Another grazed cattle on converted marshland around Seney for a few years, but he eventually gave up and returned to St. Paul.

Andrews proclaimed Cloverland for almost any kind of crop from hay, wheat, rye, and hemp, to potatoes, peas, oats, and

The Menominee Abstract and Land Company advertised Men- ominee as being, "The Leading Agricultural county of Clover- Land. Within 10 hours ride of 10,000,000 people whose needs must be supplied by the farmer. Raise what you eat. Sell what you don't eat. Your crops grow while you sleep. Good prices and best markets for the Farmer. Meno- minee County has good Lands, Markets, Schools, Churches, Roads, Sugar Factory, Canning Factory, Pickling Factory, Pack- ing Company, Cheese Factories, Creameries and Potato Ware- houses, County Agricultural School and Largest Farms to be Found in the State. Good climate and uniform rainfall."

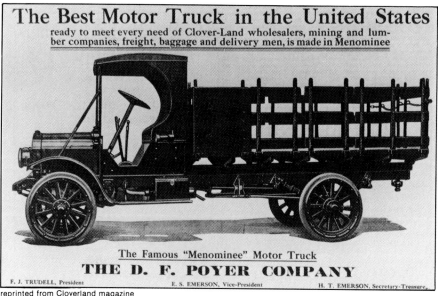

The Best Motor Truck in the United States
ready to meet every need of Clover-Land wholesalers, mining and lumber companies, freight, baggage and delivery men, is made in Menominee

The Famous "Menominee" Motor Truck
THE D. F. POYER COMPANY
F. J. TRUDELL, President   E. S. EMERSON, Vice-President   H. T. EMERSON, Secretary-Treasurer

reprinted from Cloverland magazine

barley. "Greater Cloverland is not the Garden of Eden reincarnated," he mused. "Neither does money grow on bushes. But 'the land floweth with milk and honey' for the industrious farmer, the livestock grower, the dairyman, the gardener. Nature has done her work. Man must do his share. And when man does his share in Greater Cloverland the results cannot be in doubt."

Local businessmen also joined the Cloverland effort. Ray Anderson of Marquette recalled that his ancestor, Bob Blemheuber, worked with the project. "He worked so hard promoting the area," recalls Anderson, "that he became known as Cloverland Bob."

J.Y. Canon of El Paso and Frank King of Tucson bought 25,000 acres seven miles north of Manistique where they planned to graze up to 75,000 steers. They organized a cattle company for half a million dollars and started promoting the sale of stock to purchase 50,000 additional acres.

Andrews turned from agriculture long enough to promote separate statehood for his Cloverland in 1916. "There is room in Old Glory for another star," he wrote. "*Cloverland* will be the home magazine of what may some day become the State of Superior."

In 1919, supposedly to help World War I veterans, 30,000 acres of muck land in Menominee County were surveyed for drainage and development "to make homes for the returning soldier boys."

Throughout Cloverland *magazine, advertisements for such products as Clover-Land Candy and rugged Clover-Land trucks capitalized on the separate-state theme.*

Delicious
Clover-Land Candy
There is no purer, better or more delicious Candy made anywhere in the world than right here in Clover-Land.

reprinted from Cloverland magazine

Officials of the Soo Line Railroad were also convinced by Andrews' hokum. They saw an opportunity for hog farming in the peninsula, so they equipped an exhibition car with prize-winning Duroc-Jersey hogs from the Wisconsin and Minnesota state fairs. The hog train toured all the towns along the Soo Lines in the Upper Peninsula and upper Wisconsin. During one such tour, the story developed about a farmer who was seen looking over one of the sows. When he was told that she was a frisky two-year-old that weighed in at 830 pounds, he left in disgust. "Nonsense to raise such a hog," he scoffed. "I don't know where I could ever get a bar'l big enough to scald her in." Not wishing to be outdone, the Michigan State Extension Service operated a "bull train" through the peninsula in an effort to improve the genetic base of dairy cattle and increase their milk yields.

In 1921, Andrews changed the slant of *Cloverland* magazine to tourism. Calling the Upper Peninsula the roof garden of the United States and a "vest pocket edition of almost every resort region on the globe," Andrews extolled it as a tourist's paradise and a mecca for hay fever sufferers. "To the anemic, the weak, the pallid, the listless—Cloverland is, indeed, a great out-door sanitarium." He promoted Cloverland for "the camper, the hiker, the Isaak Walton, the Daniel Boone, the swimmer, the canoe-hound."

In 1922, Andrews turned his attention to honeybees. "Just as the children of Israel looked toward the land of Canaan as a land flowing with milk and honey," he wrote, "so beekeepers of the U.S. are looking toward the Upper Peninsula as a land of honey, and just as the Israelites realized their dream, so the beekeepers of the Upper Peninsula find the nearest fulfillment of what they think to be an ideal location for their business."

By 1927, however, the truth about the rigors of U.P. agriculture was sinking in. The name Cloverland was dropped in favor of Hiawathaland. Andrews said Cloverland sounded "too agricultural" and did not adequately describe enough of the recreational advantages of the Upper Peninsula. Transportation officials quickly switched the proposed name of the new Straits ferry from Cloverland to Hiawathaland. Soon, the old name all but disappeared, along with the sheep ranchers and stump pullers, the wool-carding and fleece-lined underwear at 39 cents per suit. By the early 1930s, one-third of Michigan was tax-delinquent cutover timberland. Sheep herding had failed. The beet sugar company had gone broke. The small farm was dead, the stock market had crashed, and people were scrambling to find any work they could.

Sheep population in the peninsula dropped from 30,000 in 1920 to virtually none by 1970. In the last ten years it has grown again to a few thousand. Little 20-acre cleared farms that numbered 12,300 in 1920 had dropped by 1979 to just over 2,000. Potatoes, which occupied some 17,000 acres in 1920, occupied only one-fifth of that acreage by 1970. While the concept of Cloverland and the belief that the Upper Peninsula could become an agricultural paradise have drifted off into history, agriculture still contributes to the peninsula's income, ranking fourth in its economy. But today's farmers know more about their land, have better equipment, and are not deluded by anyone's false promises of the future. If Roger Andrews returned today, he'd find pretty tough sledding.

courtesy The Marine Corporation, Wisconsin

The Christmas Tree Ship

Each November beginning in 1887, brothers August and Herman Schuenemann took crews into the cutover areas north of Manistique and Thompson and cut Christmas trees for the Chicago market. Packing their cargo on a small schooner, they often made two runs to the big city where their fragrant spruce and balsam brought prices of 75 cents and a $1 each, depending on size. Both the cutting and the sailing were hard work, but the lure of a couple profitable voyages to close out the season was too attractive to turn down. It was a popular end-of-the-season activity among skippers, which resulted in Wisconsin and Upper Peninsula trees also showing up on the docks in Milwaukee, Detroit, and Cleveland.

By 1910, Herman was alone in the business—brother August disappeared at sea in an 1898 storm—and so Herman purchased the *Rouse Simmons* to continue the trade. He was 40 then, a jovial sort with a ruddy complexion and laughing wrinkles around his blue eyes. Although he had the reputation of being close with the dollar, Herman was an experienced sailor and was respected as a veteran captain, an honest trader, and a good family man. Sometimes Schuenemann's wife, Barbara, based in Chicago, would bring their three daughters aboard the ship for short voyages in fair weather.

The *Rouse Simmons* had even more years experience than its captain. It had been built in Milwaukee in 1868 by Allan, McClelland & Company and had compiled a steady, if not illustrious, career log in the lumber trade. The ship was 127 feet long, 27½ feet wide, and carried three masts, fore and aft rigged. Although Schuenemann was in the prime of his life, the *Rouse Simmons* had begun to show her age by late autumn of 1912 when she called at Thompson to be loaded with Christmas trees. The canvas was old and patched, the brightwork no longer glistened, the paint was most notable by its absence than its presence. But she was sturdy enough, felt Schuenemann, and he enlisted Milwaukee sailing master Charles Nelson as a partner in this Yuletide voyage. It had been a rugged season on the lakes, and the skies had scarcely cleared from an early November storm when Herman's crew began loading the seven-to-eight-foot-tall balsam and spruce. There was more bulk than weight to the cargo, so when the hold was packed full and the hatches battened, more trees were lashed on deck until the *Rouse Simmons* looked like a floating forest, green from stem to gudgeon.

There were dark clouds to the west as the loading was completed on Tuesday, November 26. Other vessels were scurrying into

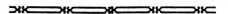

Bob Heuel rendered this painting of the Rouse Simmons, *Captain Schuenemann's "Christmas Tree Ship," under full sail.*

photo courtesy of the Marine Historical Collection, Milwaukee Public Library

the protection of the Manistique and Thompson harbors, but Herman Schuenemann knew too well that the longer he waited, the more the value of his cargo diminished. He hoped to be at his familiar station, the Clark Street bridge on the Chicago River, by the first of December, and at that time of year it took about five days to make the 300-mile trip, even in good weather. If he waited for the storm to pass it might be too late. The dozen or so lumberjacks, waiting that morning to hitch a ride back to the city, knew the dangers of felling and wedging and river driving, but had probably never experienced the awesome fury of a November storm on the Great Lakes such as they were about to face.

"Come ahead, boys!" shouted Schuenemann, and several lumberjacks clambered aboard as crew members cast off the lines and raised the ragged sails. To the east, the steam tug *Burger,* towing the schooner *Dutch Boy,* was reaching for the safety of the Manistique harbor. They had been pounded by surf and storm for hours. When the *Burger's* captain, Dennis Gallagher, spotted the *Rouse Simmons,* he couldn't believe Schuenemann was heading out into the lake, and called his crew to witness. Gallagher turned toward the harbor; the *Rouse Simmons* buried her nose in a roller and headed for open water. It was generally agreed that Schuenemann was an experienced, capable skipper. He'd survived too many storms to be otherwise. But there was also general agreement that he had shown bad judgement by setting sail that November day.

By dawn the *Rouse Simmons* had covered approximately 100 miles, but the weather was worsening and Captain Schuenemann's best option was to seek shelter in Bailey's Harbor on the eastern shore of the Door Peninsula. He might have made it, but for a sudden shifting of the wind from northwest to east. The temperature dropped, and blinding snow came pelting down. The trees on deck caught the snow and became a tremendous burden. Waves crashing over the deck coated the trees with a heavy load of ice, and water leaked through the old tarp hatch covers which added weight in the hold. It was all too much for the old *Rouse Simmons* and her veteran master. That night a huge wave caught and shook the ship, sweeping most of the deck load and two sailors overboard. Both men were lost. By noon the next day, spotters at the old United States Lifesaving Service at Kewaunee located the *Simmons* on the horizon, low in the water and flying distress signals. Through blind weather conditions, a rescue boat made an unsuccessful attempt to reach the ship. A slight break in the storm gave them a final glimpse of the old schooner encased in ice—sails in tatters—being driven southward toward Chicago with 17 people aboard.

Communication was slow in those days, and news of the *Rouse Simmons'* fate filtered back slowly. It was not until Thursday, December 5 that the *Escanaba Morning Press* carried a brief story under the headline, "Schooner is Lost." With a Chicago dateline of December 4, the story said: "That the schooner *Rouse Simmons* is in the bottom of Lake Michigan is the belief in maritime circles here today. The *Simmons* left Thompson, Schoolcraft County, Michigan for Chicago a week ago and she has not appeared here, so it is probable that she went to the bottom in the terrific storm which swept the lake last week. After a message had been received in Milwaukee that the *Simmons* was seen off Kewaunee, Wisconsin

The Rouse Simmons *was 127 feet long, 27½ feet wide, and carried three masts, fore and aft rigged.*

94

THIS IS THE TALE OF **THE CHRISTMAS SHIP!**

Chicago Sunday Tribune

Graphic Section Dec. 24, 1944

photo courtesy of Superior View, Marquette

flying distress signals, the *Tuscarora* went in search of her and nothing has been heard of her since that departure."

On December 14, the *Morning Press* printed the contents of a note, found in a bottle, believed to be the last thing written by Captain Schuenemann. It read, "Everybody good bye. Guess we are all through. Sea washed over deckload Thursday. Leaking bad. Engwald and Stade [Steve] fell overboard Thursday. God Help us."

Another bottled note, supposedly signed by mate Steve Nelson, washed ashore in 1927. It read, "These lines are written at 10:30 p.m. Schooner R.S. ready to go down about 20 miles southeast of Two Rivers point, between 15 and 20 miles offshore. All hands lashed to one line. Goodbye." The validity of the note is questioned because the message from Schuenemann indicated that Nelson (identified as Stade) had been washed overboard earlier.

Lake Michigan fishermen found their nets fouled with Christmas trees for years after the tragedy. On April 23, 1924, Captain Schuenemann's wallet, sealed so well that some of the papers inside were still legible, washed ashore near Two Rivers, Wisconsin. In 1971, Milwaukee scuba diver Kent Bellrichard found the battered wreckage of the *Rouse Simmons* in 180 feet of water about nine miles northeast of Two Rivers. The old ship was still largely intact, and divers could make out the letters on her nameplate. As final proof of the ship's identity, they brought up the bare remains of two Christmas trees that had been part of the cargo.

In 1913, buyers who came to the Clark Street bridge discovered another schooner loaded with Christmas trees. Barbara Schuenemann had hired a crew and ship, gone north again and returned with the holiday cargo. She and her daughters faithfully continued the routine until 1921 when the ship she had chartered sank before the annual November trip. That year, and ever after, the trees came by train. Barbara Schuenemann died in 1933, and for several years her daughters carried on in her place. Eventually they gave it up, and the Christmas Tree Ship, known so well to Chicago residents, passed from real life into legend.

In December, 1944, the Chicago Tribune *published this dramatic painting along with a story about the fate of the Christmas Tree Ship. It was titled "Why Chicago Missed Its Yule Trees in 1912."*

95

photo by Owen Neils, East Lansing

Sauna—The Finnish Import

Dwindling numbers of Americanized Finnish lips are currently smacking over a bowl of *viili*, a piece of *uunijuusto* or a serving of *kalakukko;* long, graceful handmade birch skis have been replaced by runty, fiberglass contemporaries; and a quiet evening tune plunked on the family *kantele* is a thing of the past. The popularity of the Finnish sauna, on the other hand, has reached new heights during the past two decades, racing throughout America under a full head of steam—which, of course, is what it contains. It is difficult to say what precipitated the present and sudden widespread acceptance of the sauna among non-believers and non-Finns, but perhaps the greatest force behind this sweaty movement has been the development of the basement sauna. Its comparatively low cost, compactness, and convenience make it ideal for town folk with small lots and zoning laws. If you have a hammer and saw, and can distinguish between them, constructing a basement sauna is within your ability.

The first sauna was probably used in the south Baltic area more than two thousand years ago, long before the Finnish tribe which constructed it had moved into the area we know as Finland. It was a crude affair, a hole dug into the side of an earthen bank in which a pile of stones was heated by an open fire. When the stones were hot and enough smoke had filtered out to permit breathing, the bather entered, threw water on the rocks, and the sauna process was under way. The steam rising from the rocks enveloped the bather, opening his pores and flowing the grime from his body on waves of sweat. This was the early *savu,* or smoke sauna. The hole-in-the-bank savu gave way to a crude log hut with a sod roof. Stone fireplaces replaced the open fires circling the pile of stones and, in time, such niceties as floors and windows were added. It was this sauna which presided in Finland for centuries, the same one which the Finnish copper miners introduced to Michigan in the 1860s. One bather remembers that preparation of the smoke sauna was no light task. The initial firing took three or four hours, by which time the dense, acrid smoke had filled the room down to knee level, and those feeding the fire had to approach on their bellies. When the pile of sauna stones was hot enough, the fire was permitted to burn out, but it was another hour before enough unneeded smoke filtered out to allow the needy family to filter in. The black, sooty walls of the savu were always ready to decorate unwary backsides, and after the water was thrown on the stones and the birch switches began their

Ahhh...there is no such thing as a quick sauna. Ample time should be allowed for the loyly, *or envelope of steam—and the thoughts it produces—to run a leisurely course. Leisure is the key to a good sauna.*

cadence, dense clouds of fly ash enveloped the bather, suggesting that he was losing ground in his effort to get clean. But eventually the rivers of sweat and pails of water turned the tide, and that luscious feeling which inspires the Finns' reverence of their beloved sauna began to creep into place. Those who are strangers to the sauna cannot comprehend such a feeling. Ah yes...

The sauna is surrounded by legend and tradition. It has been said that in ancient times the sauna was operated in three shifts, the first being attended by men and boys, the second by women and girls, and the third by the sauna fairy. Tardy bathers would skip their sauna, rather than infringe upon the fairy's privacy and risk her disfavor. An old Finnish saying emphasized that one must behave in the sauna, though naked, as one would in church, and those who violated the sanctity of the steam room would be dealt with harshly. Although men and women of all ages occasionally shared the sauna together, there was never any thought of immoral activities. In fact, obvious ogling was as much a taboo as shouting or cursing. It was what we would today call an eye-contact activity.

The impact of the sauna on the lives of the early Finns went far beyond its production of cleanliness. Midwives practiced their profession in the sauna, and the aged were frequently brought there to die: Birth and death. Engagement and bachelor saunas were held as bachelor parties are today, in one final fling before matrimony, but the wedding-eve sauna was for the bride alone. Grain was threshed in the sauna, flax was broken down in readiness for the spinning wheel, and malt was prepared for home table ale. Fish nets were dried and the catch was cured in the sauna. So were hams and bacon. And during bitter winter weather, even farm animals were sometimes permitted to share this ultimate refuge. The ancient art of cupping—the withdrawal of blood by means of suction cups fashioned from hollow cow horns—was believed to be a remedy for various circulatory disorders. It was also believed that the sauna was the only place for this practice.

Even among Finnish researchers, there are conflicting viewpoints on the benefits and perils of the sauna. Depending on which report you read, it is not recommended for the pregnant woman, or

An important part of the sauna is the cooling-off period. It can be accomplished by taking a shower, or by jumping into the nearest snow bank or a hole in the ice as the brave bather, pictured below, has done. Another important sauna tradition involves being flogged with a vihta. *It is made from birch twigs and leaves that are bound with a pliable birch branch, below right, dipped in cold water, and laid briefly on hot sauna stones to be softened. Beating the body gently with a vihta aids circulation and hastens perspiration. It is considered to be as personal as a toothbrush.*

photo courtesy of David M. Frimodig, Laurium

photo courtesy of David M. Frimodig, Laurium

it is excellent for all stages of pregnancy. The suggestion that people who have suffered a stroke or heart attack should not take a sauna conflicts with one clinical test which determined that people who continued taking saunas following a heart attack enjoyed a longer life span than those who didn't. It is often suggested that elderly people stay away from saunas, but the late Mathilda Weidelman was still enjoying her weekly saunas at the age of 101.

It's possible the early smoke sauna contributed to the high rate of respiratory diseases among the Finns, but residual fears that tuberculosis is routinely served with the steam are totally unfounded. Also not true is an oft-heard claim that the sauna will cure the common cold. There's no doubt in my mind, however, that the sauna does help to loosen congestion during the final stages of a respiratory infection. I once paid 20 bucks to a prominent nose and throat specialist in exchange for his suggestion that I take my sinuses to a sauna. Another bit of fiction is that the sauna removes excess lard by the ton. Sure, the initial loss of body fluids makes the scales smile in your favor, but once the lost fluids have been replaced with cool beverages, as they should be, the needle quickly jumps back to more familiar numbers.

There's no doubt that the sauna is good for the complexion, as the faces of both men and women on the streets of Helsinki or Vasa will quickly prove. The flow of perspiration flushes grime and bacteria from the skin's pores and the high temperatures help unplug the openings of the sebaceous glands, thus preventing the formation of blackheads...a real boon to acne-prone teenagers.

How do you take a sauna? First of all, while the stones are heating and the thermometer begins its journey skyward, you must decide at what temperature you wish to get involved. The answer lies somewhere between 135 and 220 degrees F., depending upon age, health, experience and, most of all, preference. Most experts agree that the minimum sauna temperature should be 175 degrees, but I would suggest that amateurs step in a little sooner, working up gradually to personal optimum temperatures. In a totally dry sauna, the bather simply sweats in hot, dry air free of steam, while in the more common humid sauna, water is thrown on the hot stones to

Saunas were so much a part of a Finn's life that community saunas were built to accommodate those who did not have their own. When men and women shared the same sauna, which was not uncommon, they were expected to behave, even though naked, as one would in church.

photo courtesy of David M. Frimodig, Laurium

produce a rapid sensation of heat. Theoretically, bathers who are slow to perspire should select the humid sauna, while those who sweat readily and profusely usually prefer the dry sauna.

There is no such thing as taking a "quick sauna." Ample time should be allowed for the *loyly,* or envelope of steam, and the thoughts it produces, to run their leisurely course—leisure is the key to a good sauna. Under no circumstances should the sauna become a competitive event to determine who can take the most steam. Such competition is unpleasant, unhealthy, and real dumb.

Properly taken, a sauna consists of a series of individual steps, beginning with the initial perspiring done in dry heat. All leading authorities agree that during this sitting, no water should be thrown on the hot stones, but it's been my experience that excessive heat and dryness do not always make the pores cry. On such occasions, a preliminary shower or sponging down of the body may trigger the flow of perspiration, as might a pail of water sloshed on the wall. If you don't mind contradicting worldwide authorities, a premature dipper of water on the hot stones works equally well.

An old Finnish saying, *"Lammin ja lysti kun napakin savuaa"* is a good general guideline in determining when the steam room has reached its optimum temperature and humidity: "Warmly pleasant when the navel smokes." (Indeed!) When a good amount of perspiration has been achieved, the first cooling in a lake, pool, shower or breeze should follow. If privacy and courage are available, a roll in the snow cools best of all, but beware of a crust! When you have fully cooled off, it's time to return to the sauna, and it's also time to feed a dipper of water to the hot stones, in exchange

These men are emerging clean, refreshed, and relaxed from an underground sauna.

photo courtesy of David M. Frimodig, Laurium

for that first blast of loyly. Despite claims that vaporized wine will dispel sauna claustrophobia, water is the only liquid which should be thrown on the hot sauna stones. It takes a moment for the hot vapor to reach the top bench, so don't offer the stones seconds or thirds until you've felt their reaction to the first dipper. This is also the step where the birch *vihta* is brought into play, but not until it is dipped in cold water and laid briefly on the sauna stones, to soften the leaves and twigs. The vihta is used to beat the body, arms, and legs for the purpose of aiding circulation and hastening perspiration. When dipped in cold water and held against the face, it is also a valuable aid to breathing during those brief occasions when the loyly becomes a bit much. Incidently, the vihta is considered to be as personal as a toothbrush and should never be shared. These alternate steps of "taking steam" and cooling off may be repeated as often as you wish or as long as waiting bathers will tolerate.

The next step is to wash, and if you're restricted to bucket-bathing in the steam room, don't overlook the buddy system with its "I'll wash your back, if you'll wash mine" philosophy. After a brief return to the steam room to warm up and reflect upon your good fortune, and a final dip or shower, the cooling-off period begins. It is during this step that amateurs often go astray by trying to speed up the process, inevitably winding up with clammy underwear and an even damper enthusiasm for a return engagement. It takes experience to know when your post-sauna pores have completely returned to normal, and patience to wait at least that long before getting dressed. Ideally, the cooling should take place outside in a blissful mingling of bare bottoms and balmy breezes, but most suburbs have archaic laws against such public ecstasy. Because the body will have lost a lot of fluids, it is important that it be reimbursed as soon as possible.

For those readers facing their debut on the top bench, I offer these reminders: Practice moderation in temperature, humidity, and conduct; scrub your partner's back; and don't pull on your drawers 'till your pores close. "*Hyvia loyloya*"—good sauna!

This log smoke sauna or "savu" was the most prevalent style in Finland for centuries, and was introduced to Michigan by Finnish copper miners in the 1860s.

painting by Peder Kitti, Lac La Belle

102

When A Kitchen Really Was

The kitchen was the heart of the home a generation or two ago, and for those who enthusiastically carry on traditions established by parents and grandparents, it still is. I admit to an eater's expertise. As the youngest of eight children and twenty-five college students who thrived on the culinary talents of a widowed mother with one small kitchen range, I should be qualified to make this introduction to Upper Peninsula kitchens and the wonderful things that occurred therein.

What was so different about those early kitchens which produced such special meals and memories? There certainly wasn't much appeal to their bare hardwood floors whose ever-widening cracks with tiny caches of food were totally inaccessible to broom or beagle. And despite their current price tags, the traditional round oak kitchen tables were not considered the least bit pretentious a half-century or so ago—except, perhaps, immediately after the old blue-and-white checkered oilcloth was removed and a new one was tacked into place. There was something about a new oilcloth which shouted elegance. But that impression was usually burned away by a hot pan within a week.

Then there was the massive oak icebox that hulked in a corner away from the stove. Now there was a monster whose entire life was dedicated to aggravating people! For one thing, block ice was never created in sizes that would fit iceboxes and each delivery involved much custom chiseling and showers of ice particles in every direction. Only the family dog appreciated such chilly debris—in hot weather he could be relied upon to handle most of the clean up chores. The icebox continued its deviltry throughout the week, habitually overflowing the drain pan the instant it was ignored. Even those homes which boasted a melt-pipe to the basement were not exempt from periodic floods, for icebox drains seemed to choke voluntarily on bits of lettuce or celery greens. For some reason, ice blocks always melted faster in the back, and food items placed on the top surface eventually slid behind, out of sight. It was extremely difficult to remove a thirty-pound block of ice, retrieve the elusive food, and return the ice without collecting a couple of purple toes. And, of course, there were secret nooks in every icebox which collected stray bits of cheese or pork chop that were never missed until the iceman was a day or two late with his delivery.

When the Upper Peninsula Power Company first began selling kitchen appliances, any icebox was worth two dollars toward a new

The cookstove often did double duty on chilly winter mornings when its talent for warming backsides took precedence over accommodating hunger pangs.

Manila Gipp's
Stollen

Makes 4 loaves

Sponge: 3 cups flour, 2 cups potato water, 2 pkgs. dry yeast. Soften yeast in ½ cup warm water. Boil 1 medium potato in about 1½ cups water until soft. Mash potato in water, add more water if necessary to make 1½ cups. When lukewarm, add to yeast and stir in the flour. Beat well. It should be quite thick. Let rise about ½ hour or until sponge is almost to top of bowl. Then add the following ingredients, according to the directions:

1 cup Crisco
½ cup butter, softened
3 eggs
about 6½ cups flour
1½ tablespoons salt
2 cups sugar
1 oz. lemon extract
1 cup dark raisins
1 cup white raisins
2 slices candied pineapple
3 oz. red and green candied cherries
½ teaspoon nutmeg

To the sponge, add the sugar, nutmeg, and salt. Mix well. Then add the eggs and beat well. Add the flour and shortening alternately by hand. After about half the flour has been added, stir in the lemon extract and the fruit, which has been floured. Continue adding flour and shortening until dough does not stick to bottom of bowl, and it is coming off your hand easily. Cover and let rise about 3 to 4 hours, until your finger imprint stays in dough.

To make each loaf, take ¼ of the dough and pat on breadboard till approximate size of bread pan. Cut each piece into 3 lengthwise strips, but leave attached at one end. Braid and put into greased pans. Cover with cloth and allow to rise about 1 hour. When ready to put in oven, brush beaten egg over top and sprinkle with sugar. Bake at 325 degrees for 45 minutes, then about 10 to 15 minutes at 350 degrees. When done, remove from pans and place on rack to cool.

electric unit. The company hauled the old ice-eater to the dump, besides. Most folks were well satisfied with the transaction, for when purchased new, their Michigan "refrigerator" with the solid brass hardware had cost only about $10 at Sears, Roebuck and Company. Who would have dreamed that 50 or 60 years later the going price for that good ol' icebox would be $200 to $300?

The five-foot Hoosier Kitchen Kabinet was, for years, the only storage facility in the kitchen, but it did very nicely. "Just a few minutes of pleasant occupation and—presto! the meal's ready! That's how the Hoosier can end kitchen drudgery!" An overly enthusiastic claim, perhaps, but there's no doubt that this cabinet with its built-in flour sifter, sugar and coffee dispensers, retractable counter top, and multiple cubbyholes had universal appeal. It was a standard accessory in most kitchens. True, its modern counterpart has a far greater capacity for storing things, but heck, that's why pantries were invented. Ah, that tantalizing pantry with its built-in fragrance of cooling bread and fresh pies, its unreachable, kid-proof shelves, and that big cookie jar with the controlled inventory of ginger snaps! Dead-end pantries were off-limits, but a pantry with through-traffic was an irresistible challenge. With a little practice, handfuls of goodies could be pocketed without breaking stride!

Without question, the old wood range was the kitchen's heart and soul. Jet black and lavishly adorned with shiny nickel bands, handles, and door frames, it was a beautiful thing to see. Its porcelain-lined reservoir assured a continuous supply of hot water, and the overhead warming oven preserved supper's integrity for the breadwinner returning from field, forest, or a late shift at the mine.

Veteran wood stove cooks were stoking professionals who always knew the precise number and arrangement of hardwood sticks in the firebox for the current fare. Once the range cooled off from its supper chores, the nickel-trimmed baseburner in the parlor assumed full responsibility for heating the house. With careful banking of wood or soft coal, it might burn throughout the night, but long before dawn it ceased to contribute to upstairs comfort. Multiple quilts kept bodies warm from then on, and shedding that cozy cocoon in the morning involved great courage and precision. With the first gray of dawn, one ear ventured just far enough into the chill to pick up the encouraging sound of shaking grates coming from the kitchen. Although the primary responsibility of the wood range involved groceries, there were many frosty mornings when its talent for warming backsides took precedence over its ability to accommodate hunger pangs. After an educated pause to let the morning fire gain authority, kids catapulted from bed and, with the clothes of the day clutched in their arms, they homed in on the smell of bacon and the radiant warmth of the wood range.

If this was the day to change underwear, thoughtful mothers had it preheating on nails behind the range, next to the black, knitted tights still clammy from yesterday's "snow angels." Seemingly, a body couldn't get close enough to that delicious source of heat, but those who faced away from the range while bending into their long johns eventually learned this was not always true. Strangely enough, new blisters on the behind which decimated attention spans during the morning's geography lesson hardly ever disrupted afternoon sledding programs.

painting by Peder Kitti, La Belle

Besides cold kids and underwear, the kitchen range worked
wonders on wet boots, wet dogs, and the family wash. Monday
morning was easily distinguished by the assorted pieces of dirty
clothes on the kitchen floor, waiting their turn in the boiler on top
of the range. The clothes simply *had* to be boiled in a bluing solution before the scrub, wring, and rinse routine took place, and every
schoolboy made as one of his shop projects a long, tapered clothes
fork for transferring boiled clothes to waiting tubs.

During winter months, trenches were dug beneath the clothes-
lines out back, but freeze-dried long johns frequently had to stand
in kitchen corners a spell before they could be folded or hung on
kitchen lines to complete the drying process. When storms raged on
washdays, the entire wash was festooned about the kitchen and wet
slaps were common to all but the agile. In Rudy Fink's home, the
smell of brown soap, boiling clothes and drying underwear was in-
variably blended with another traditional washday aroma, boiled
cabbage—a bouquet which predominated until midweek, at least.

Laundry rinse water was assigned extra duty on the kitchen
floor, and the largest washtub was hauled out again on Saturday
night for the weekly kitchen baths. Aino Liikala recalls that the seven

*The kitchen doubled as a laundry
room on washday. When the
weather was nasty, the wet clothes
were festooned about the kitchen
to dry. Laundry rinse water was
often put to a second use on the
kitchen floor, and the largest
washtub was brought out again on
Saturday night for the family's
weekly baths. On the following
pages are pictures of some tasty
Upper Peninsula foods including
pasties, prune and apricot tarts,
breads, and cookies, and a few
favorite recipes.*

105

Anna Backman Kitti's Frugt Supper

1 pound mixed dried fruits
(apricots, prunes, raisins, apples,
peaches)
2½ quarts water
1 stick cinnamon
1 cup sugar
2 tablespoons cornstarch
2 tablespoons cold water
1 lemon and 1 orange, sliced, if
    desired

Simmer the dried fruits in the
water with the cinnamon stick until
the fruits are tender, about an hour.
Add sugar, stirring until dissolved,
and simmer a few minutes. Dissolve
cornstarch in the 2 tablespoons cold
water and add to the fruit, stirring
until soup has thickened slightly and
is clear. Serve either warm or cool,
with light cream or whipped cream if
desired.

Anna Backman Kitti's Kropsua

3 eggs
2 cups milk
1 cup flour
½ teaspoon salt
½ cup butter or oleo

Melt the butter in a 9 x 13 inch pan
till sizzling but not brown. Mix other
ingredients only enough to be well
blended. Pour into pan and bake in
preheated 400-degree oven for 35 to
45 minutes. Cut in desired size pieces
and serve at once, using berry sauces
or syrup if it is a breakfast dish, or
with fresh berries and whipped cream
for the ultimate in desserts.

Finns' Rieska

3 cups white flour
1½ cups graham or rye flour
1 tablespoon salt
¼ cup sugar
1 tablespoon baking powder
½ teaspoon baking soda
2 cups buttermilk
½ cup melted oleo or butter

Mix all ingredients together quickly, as for baking powder biscuits.
Round up on lightly floured board.
Knead lightly, just a few strokes.
Divide in two pieces and roll or pat
each to about ¾ inch thick. Bake on
ungreased baking sheet in preheated
425 degree oven about 25 minutes.

photo courtesy of David M. Frimodig, Laurium

kids in her family were usually processed in the same tub of water,
although the sequence was rotated periodically by popular demand.

In many early Upper Peninsula homes, the cracks which invited winter cold were just as efficient in admitting summer heat.
With an assist from the kitchen range, summer temperatures often
soared twenty degrees above bearable. Woe unto the entire family
when a prolonged heat wave coincided with the garden harvest and
the long days of canning which followed. Little could be done except to shed as many layers as the propriety of the day permitted
and keep noses to the screens—penance for having a mother with a
green thumb and empty pantry shelves.

Those who had summer kitchens were more fortunate. For
such town folks, that hot weather retreat was usually located in a
corner of the basement away from the coal bin. The accessories
were basic, consisting of a small wood stove, table and sink, but it
sure wore well on those sweltering days when the upstairs kitchen
range was granted leave from normal chores.

Those who lived on a farm or had a little acreage on the edge of
town often located their summer kitchen in a separate building, a
quick dash away from main kitchen supplies and utensils. Some
were rather elaborate, with separate rooms for cooking and eating,
and cots along the walls for noontime snoozes or humid nights.
Others were more simply furnished, but the common feature of all
rural summer kitchens was screened windows on four sides. With
fragrant breezes wafting in from the clover field, supper could be a
delightful experience, and toil-whetted appetites responded enthusiastically to the occasion. But nobody gets nostalgic about those inevitable evenings when the breezes passed through the barn before
enveloping the summer kitchen.

Throughout the years, well-meaning children have pooled their
money to buy Grandma a spanking new gas or electric range, only
to discover that it did not replace the old wood range, but merely
joined it, side by side. If they had slipped in unannounced between
scheduled family reunions, they might have been surprised to see
the sturdy old black range still presiding over most kitchen affairs.

Grocery stores today are lined with huge, economy-size

packages of everything, but they look like individual servings compared to yesterday's bulk acquisitions for the kitchen. Everybody had a vegetable garden, and the harvest was measured in bushels, not pounds or bunches. Wild fruit enjoyed great prominence among the shelves of preserves, and although all kids were obliged to join in the harvest, it was considered a fun outing, with a lot of good lunch, friendly competition, and when-ma-wasn't-lookin' horseplay. Sometimes empty powder boxes from the mine were rigged into backpacks, and in a plump patch of blueberries a good picker might fill it two or three times during the day.

Even store-bought commodities came in large portions. Some families had their milk delivered in neat little gallon containers, but Eino Pihlaja always brought ours in a five-gallon can which he emptied into two large bread pans on our kitchen table. The cream was skimmed off with a large spoon for special use and the remainder was transferred to jars and bottles of various sizes for convenient storage in icebox or cellar. I don't recall that any milk was discarded for aging ungracefully, but there were a few glasses toward the end of the week which should have been.

Dry toast from the local bakery resembled large frankfurter buns sliced horizontally and were sold for $4.00 a barrel. Carl Liikala recalls that kids always preferred the rounded half of the toast, and after the barrel was half empty, it was not unusual to see a pair of legs protruding from the barrel as their owner probed for one of the coveted "boats" near the bottom. In Fred Trathen's youth, one of the exciting pastimes on a winter's evening was to snitch a half-frozen rutabaga from the cellar bin and gnaw on it until "your teeth started to bleed!"

Art Coppo recalls that he could always tell when kitchen chores were under control because that's when Grandma would don a clean apron, pour a fresh cup of tea, and sigh into the kitchen chair by the window. More often than not, the pause was only a cup of tea long and then it was time to think about supper. Grandmas and kitchens were perpetually busy in those days.

Traditionally, nostalgia distorts reality and sentiment thrives best on pleasant memories. Old family kitchens probably had far more drawbacks than virtues, and yet there persists this feeling that things just aren't as good as they used to be in the food department. A 1915 issue of the *Keweenaw News* applauded the virtues of the Upper Peninsula kitchen in a manner which left no doubt about the importance of its role, relative to anything:

"As a means of promoting efficiency and saving labor, nothing can be more important than the study of the Upper Peninsula kitchen. It is the workshop in which thousands of dollars worth of material, more or less raw, is made into a manufactured product which goes directly into thousands of mouths and sustains thousands of human brains and bodies. Upon the quality of this manufactured product depends the welfare of society. Good food makes happy homes, keeps families united, accomplishes wonders in keeping men from drink and children from breaking down under the stress of modern education. Upon it hangs the issue of life or death. The kitchen, then, should need no advocate and no defender. It is the most important room in the house."

I'll toast to that!

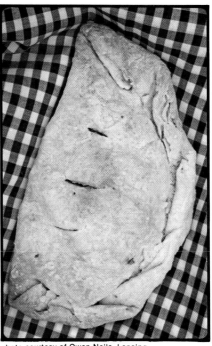
photo courtesy of Owen Neils, Lansing

Pasties

Pastry for four pasties
  1 cup finely grated suet
  ¾ cup shortening,
    (part lard, part oleo)
  ½ tablespoon salt
  3 cups pastry flour

Mix with fingers until shortening particles are about the size of small peas. Add ice water gradually and moisten until pastry stays firmly together. You may, instead, substitute your favorite pastry recipe for the suet recipe.

Ingredients for four large pasties
  2 lbs. lean pork and beef,
    cut in ½ inch cubes
  2 cups onions, sliced or diced fine
  1 cup rutabagas,
    sliced or diced fine
  1 cup potatoes, sliced or diced fine

If desired, you may omit the pork, but add a small pat of oleo or butter if beef is very lean. Roll pastry out and use a nine-inch plate as a pattern to cut the dough into a circle. Fill with alternate layers of meat and vegetables, beginning and ending with meat. Salt and pepper to taste. Fold pastry in the middle, press firmly together, crimp near the top, and prick with fork three times to let it know who's boss. Bake one hour at 400 degrees F. and keep in mind that a two-pasty eater is a cook's biggest compliment!

107

photo by Childs Art Gallery courtesy of Superior View, Marquette

Coping With Snow

In October, usually, the first snow falls steady on the northland, whispering teasing promises of more to come. White fluffy flakes drift lazily from the skies, then turn to whirl off through the trees or to flatten themselves in wet globby flakes against Upper Peninsula windowpanes. The first snow surprises autumn leaves, still blushing red on trees in Michigan's Copper Country. It races madly down the Keweenaw, beating Halloween to the pumpkin. It transforms the hillsides and forests into wonderlands, with frozen garlands tying the pines together, white blankets settled everywhere on the land, icy sculptures silencing the waterfalls, the streams, the rivers, sometimes even lulling rough old Lake Superior to sleep. Citizens of the Copper Country—from Houghton to Copper Harbor—live with this snowfall, applaud its loveliness, curse its driving fierceness, then bemoan the day it disappears.

Old-timers reminisce about the great snows of yesterday, while those not so old talk about the Big Snow of 1978-79. It piled up the annual average of 235 inches by January, then kept right on coming. By the time winter tabulations were complete, the official measuring station at Delaware, toward the tip of the Keweenaw, boasted 390.6 inches for the year, topping all previous records for the Copper Country. Think of it, 390.6 inches! That's more than 32 feet of snow in one winter! *Talk about coping!*

Still, for the people of the Keweenaw, snow never comes too soon. "I don't mind shoveling snow in January," says Armando Zei of Laurium, with good logic. "It's just that much less we have to shovel in February." Shovelers often carve tunnels to their doors. Reinforced with posts and stout boards, such tunnels eliminate daily shoveling of the nightly snowfalls. These entrances also resemble the underground adits, or tunnels, of the early copper mines, mines which brought settlers to the area more than a century ago. Those who don't tunnel under the snow usually go over it. Come November, they get busy preparing portable wooden sidewalks to erect three or four feet *above* the snow! Such sidewalks will allow a person to stride confidently all the way from a doorway to the cleared roadway beyond, with just a few short steps at street level. On snowy days (what days aren't?) a quick whisk of the broom along these raised wooden walks and the path is clear once again—for the moment. Some of these sidewalks stretch around the corners of houses. Some are more than a hundred feet in length, such as that of the Sacred Heart Church in Calumet.

This scene was shot during the 1890s on a street in Ishpeming. When the sidewalks were shoveled clean, folks who had snowshoed to town simply tucked their snowshoes into a nearby snowbank and went about their business. When errands were finished, the snowshoes were ready to be strapped on again for an easy trek home.

Drivers will find parking meters stationed against the buildings, well away from the street, because they would normally be buried in snow and could be chopped off by passing snowplows. Besides, nobody would dig down to put in their nickel. Car antennas are longer here, too, and they wear bright flags on top to signal an approach at intersections piled high with snow. Just backing out of a driveway can be an experience. Eight-foot flagged posts identify mailbox locations for snowblower operators. Shovelers walk up the drifts to reach their groaning rooftops, then shovel off three feet of snow—sometimes uphill! Everywhere in the peninsula, roofs are built stronger to withstand this weighty annual adornment. Kids slide from garage roofs onto drifts banked against the side. Three-foot-wide Finnish snow scoops—most people down below have never seen one—are manned by everyone, including kids and senior citizens, partially for the fun of being outside, partially for the exercise. Mummied in clothing from head to toe, these youngsters and oldsters shuffle their scoops back and forth like soldiers digging trenches, stopping to puff and chat, watching more snow clouds gathering in the west. "If I don't shovel every day, I get a headache," says one. "Give her tar paper, let her snow."

Work goes on despite the snow. Plows growl along roadways long before daylight peeks through the latest flurry. They are out, in fact, at any time of day or night up here because it snows continually. Almost everyone who owns a car plugs it into an overnight electrical connection to assure that it will start easily in the morning. Every back seat hosts a shovel. There's never a traffic delay when crossing the Portage Canal lift bridge after November; the only signs of traffic below are snowmobile trails, ski lines, and snowshoe tracks. Somehow, airplanes operating from the Houghton County Airport maintain regular arrival and departure schedules. Of course the landing strips are kept clear by large snowblowers, but there's another wrinkle that helps keep those planes on time, and that's Nathan Ruonavaara's "airplane broom." Ruonavaara devised a 14-foot-long broom to sweep airplane wings and fuselages clear of snow. That hastens de-icing procedures and assures pilots of scheduled takeoffs.

Those first snows of October may be fickle, but Copper Coun-

photo by Childs Art Gallery, courtesy of Superior View, Marquette

try folks turn ten years old again when snow settles down to stay. By mid-November, at least, hockey rinks, ski slopes and trails, snowmobile runs, and skating rinks know no age limit. Toddlers taking their first steps are just as welcome as oldsters listing to right or left from 80 years of life in this region.

Then of course there's skiing. So *much* skiing, both cross-country and downhill, and down ski jumps, and stories on stories about people who climb on the boards in this region and whisk off in one direction or another...so many stories.

Beyond skiing, there's kids at play. Snow and ice give birth to kids at play. Snow comes down and kids sprout on the streets like mushrooms in a wet meadow. Mittened elves they are, encased in zippered puffy suits, chooks pulled down to their eyebrows, bright scarves twirled around their necks. Everybody knows what chooks are. All the kids up here have them. Some spell the word chuckes, or chucks, but no one in the Keweenaw does. A chook is a stocking cap that pulls down to protect neck, ears, and most of the head. Research by Gregory A. Peet of Sault Ste. Marie revealed that our word *chook* is a corruption of the French-Canadian *Tuque,* which is a "winter cap consisting of a knitted bag tapered and closed at both ends, worn with one end tucked into the other."

Anyway, kids everywhere up here have chooks and skates, and wear both at recess, at noontime, and again after school, as they slip and slide off across the ice on big brother's hand-me-down skates, or flash along on shiny new models needed each fall because of growing feet. How many new pairs of skates appear under how many Christmas trees in the Keweenaw each year? Lots and lots, you may be sure. Snowmobiles are popular, too. The Keweenaw enjoys an average snowmobile season from mid-November through early April. Copper Country folks find plenty of time to explore the more than 100 miles of uninterrupted marked and groomed forest trails or, tiring of those, they may string off on another 200 miles of ungroomed trails. Others are content merely with a brisk walk—carefully stopping at corners, however, to peer around eight-foot snowbanks for oncoming cars.

Michigan Technological University students at Houghton use the snow to their advantage during February carnival time. As soon

photo courtesy of Department of Natural Resources, Rose Lake

The wide snowplow, far left, was used to clear roads in Marquette County during the 1920s. Wooden snow rollers such as the one pictured at left, were used by loggers, skiers, and other travelers to pack the snow into trails, rather than scrape it away.

111

photo courtesy of Alger County Historical Society

as Christmas is past, the various clubs, living units, and social groups at the university start hoarding mountains of snow, carting it in, piling it up. Imagine, *hoarding snow*! When they have enough, they begin to sculpture it into elaborate creations that sometimes stretch a block long. Human figures, animals, symbols from mythology, or scenes from well-known movies—all stand in frozen sculpted form a hundred times life-size. The night before these creations are judged for their detail and beauty, the whole campus stays awake while students carve the finishing touches on scenes from fantasy, book, and screen. Every student resident hall, fraternity, and campus organization in Houghton and Hancock sprouts ghouls and goblins looming from the lawn, or princesses crying in distress from 20-foot-high castle turrets. More than 100 such statues normally greet the judges and the morning sun.

Adventure and a love of fishing provide another method of coping with the Upper Peninsula winter. Anglers are lured by cold temperatures and thickening ice onto lakes and quiet bays tucked along the Keweenaw and Superior shores. With an ice drill, they cut holes through to open water below, then arrange their tip-up gear and sit down to wait behind a makeshift wind screen or heavy coat collar. Some take to snowmobiles, crossing the ice from shore to fishing shacks. Inside those shacks they heat up stoves to ward off outside cold, then sip hot coffee or warm wine to pacify the cold inside. Meanwhile, beneath the icy floor, fish contemplate the baited hook and sometimes indulge.

Not everyone takes to the outside, however, even when temperatures reach a balmy 20 degrees in the sun. Some folks are content to watch the snow from a window, with a good book, a bright afghan tucked around their knees, and an extra log banking the fire. Cooks in the Copper Country are at their best in the winter

Never let a little snow get in your way! On a street in Ishpeming, shoveling snow also offered an opportunity to chat with passersby.

112

photo courtesy of Marquette County Historical Society

too, using dozens of old country recipes handed down by pioneers. Finnish, Cornish, Italian, French, Polish, German, Slavic, Swedish, Norwegian—there are more recipes in heads than in books up here, and it seems they all produce luscious hot dishes filled with fruity, meaty, vegee aromas that steam up kitchen windows and hoist ski-induced appetites to record levels. The winter may howl outside, but indoors all's right with the world.

In mid-March, however, it's time to say goodbye, and folks from up and down the Keweenaw gather at Delaware for their farewell salute to winter. *Heikki Lunta* day is celebrated here with bonfires and picnics, with old man winter himself (in the form of a local resident wearing the appropriate costume) making a grand appearance. Dressed in winter garb with ice crusted heavily on his beard, *Heikki Lunta,* the Finnish God of Snow, stalks from the hardwood forests for a day of fun.

But though the residents may say farewell, winter may not decide to leave for another month, hanging on like the guest who came to dinner—and stayed...and stayed... and stayed. You would think that the people of the Upper Peninsula would have their fill after nearly seven months of snow; however, a few of them look skeptically at the approaching spring. "I'd like winter to hang around awhile longer," says Wayne Pietila wistfully, "but everyone else seems to want it to go, so I suppose I'd better go along with it."

Some things haven't changed much up here in the last many years. In winter, you'll still find clean clothes drying in warm attics and kitchens, and rag rugs thrown across cold floors. Soggy mittens still drip and steam next to the stove. And winter eventually passes, with everyone coping in their own way to use the cold days, to survive the snow and ice, and to make the long nights and short days not only liveable but fun.

When the snow fell and Hewett Grocery had a delivery to make, the horses were hitched to a sleigh and business carried on as usual.

photo by Peter Oikarinen, Calumet

114

Homemade Fun

Baffled observers of Upper Peninsula folks sometimes ask "What do you people *do* up there?" It's obvious, isn't it? In winter we shovel snow and in summer we swat mosquitoes. During the spring and fall we rest up for swatting and shoveling...

Actually, there's just a *bit* more activity than that. Name a traditional outdoors experience and you'll discover it here. Take a deep breath and recite this list: hunting, trapping, fishing, hiking, swimming (yes, even frigid Lake Superior has been known to "warm" up,) canoeing, sailing, scuba diving, camping (there are 17 state parks, Isle Royale National Park and Pictured Rocks National Lakeshore, and thousands of acres of national and state forest lands,) bicycling, bird watching, rock collecting, berry picking (including the thimbleberry, found elsewhere only in Maine,) all forms of skiing, skating, snowshoeing, snowmobiling, and more.

But leave it to Upper Peninsula folks to also invent their own forms of recreation and entertainment. For example, if you're in Bete Grise on the Keweenaw Peninsula on January 1st, you won't believe what's happening—grown men in swimming suits dashing over snowbanks and into icy Lake Superior. Why? "It's something different, something to do," says Jerry Abramson, the polar bear ringleader of these hardy (some would say foolhardy) men. Every New Year's Day since 1972, regardless of temperature or weather conditions, he's leaped into the lake. He even manages to coerce new recruits every year. Few of them repeat the experience, but Jerry hasn't missed a January, and has even done a bit of swimming at least once each month for 23 months in a row. He claims the water feels coldest in April or May. On December 23, 1975, he and a friend swam for an hour and a half. Witnesses will confirm that they took only a few short breaks on shore. The air temperature was an abnormally scorching 40 degrees. On January 1, 1979, conditions weren't as favorable. With temperatures in the low teens, Jerry could stay in for only two minutes. The coldest New Year's temperature was eight below zero. Even so, the 40 degree difference between air and water feels refreshing "...until you get out of the water. Then it feels like you've been hit by a six-foot meat tenderizer."

Less rigorous, but just as crazy, is a sport that I've dubbed "driftbusting." Blizzard winds can sculpt thick ribs of snow, up to five feet high—and even thicker—across winter roads. The object of a driftbuster is to drive from point A to unseeable point B

Jerry Abramson goes for a swim in Lake Superior every New Year's Day. He selects a location along the beach at Bete Grise because it's one of the few places where there usually isn't any ice on the water. In the photo at left, that's Jerry on the right and another polar bear, Don Hahn, on the left. The "stuff" in the foreground isn't sand, it's snow!

115

photo courtesy of Family Inn, Newberry

photo courtesy of Janice Gerred, Lansing

through these looming snowdrifts, during or just after a storm. To qualify as a driftbuster, participants must attack billowing snowbanks that would cause the timid driver to stay at home, the sane driver to go back home, and the foolish driver to get hopelessly stuck. Of course, there must be *some* chance of breaking through, and the drifts, if menacing, are scouted before the attempt is made. I've seen four-wheel drives, VW's, and old Chevys careening through the snow like playful beagles. I've also seen the inevitable shoveling and cursing. It's another calculated adventure to fight off the sometimes dismal drudgery of the long winters.

Another winter enterprise, dreamed up by eight co-graduates of Escanaba High School, occurs in and around the caves on the Stonington Peninsula in Delta County. Each February for the past several years, regardless of the weather, these men have gathered to have "fun" camping and frolicking in the snow. They snowshoe, ice fish, play football, and generally enjoy each others' company. When not physically active, they huddle round a fire in the protection of a cave. One year, temperatures plummeted below zero; another year a blizzard blasted them—it took a mile of shoveling to get their cars free. Their yearly tradition is strong. Tom Timler even had written into his marriage contract that he be given freedom from marital obligations during every first weekend in February.

These ventures aren't for everyone, but there *are* some unique events that anyone can attend. In addition to traditional lumberjack contests, the Log Jam-Boree in Ewen has two strange competitions—pulp log and chain saw throwing. "Anyone who's had trouble with their chain saw in the woods can identify with these contests," says sympathetic Dan Ojala, a Ewen resident who initiated the Jam-Boree idea. The record holder of both contests, burly Brian Maki, hurled his awkward, battered, hated chain saw 46 feet, and the 100-inch long stick of pulpwood 58.5 feet. The women's records in both of those events are held by Janice Greeno who has tossed the chain saw 22 feet, and the pulp log 28 feet.

Throwing objects seems to be very popular with Upper Peninsulites. So many stones have been removed from rocky fields, so many logs cleared, and so many mine rocks hurled into "poor-rock" cars that it's only natural that the offspring of these pioneers are still compulsively flinging objects about. In Gulliver,

Above is one of the entries in Newberry's St. Bernard Parade. Snowshoeing and dogsledding, above right, provided rigorous winter entertainment in the early days of the Upper Peninsula, just as they do today.

116

photo courtesy of Ski Hall of Fame, Ishpeming

people seem to have inherited this genetic trait. There, descendents of Scots—and anyone else strong enough—compete in the Highland Games patterned after the traditional Scottish games. There is a cabor (log) toss, hammer throw, and stone toss while a pipe and drum band inspires rivals to glorious deeds.

If the heavy Scottish stone toss is too strenuous, you can try Mackinac Island where a more refined stone throw occurs. The International Open Stone-Skipping Contest is sponsored each year by the Lake Superior State College-based Stone Skippers and Kerplunking Club. Approximately 500 skippers annually assemble to hear the traditional opening cry: "Let he who is without frisbee cast the first stone!" Each contestant is then allowed six sidearm flips. "There's nothing fantastic about my form," says one of the three world-record holders, Warren Klope. "The selection of the stone is my secret." Klope's record 24 skips made waves in stone-skipping circles in 1975. His effort won a 75-pound rock as first prize, along with a year's supply of famous Mackinac Island fudge.

The stone-skipping club is an offshoot of the Unicorn Hunter's (or Quester's) Club. The organization is "open to anyone, anywhere, who is prepared to follow a dream," says poet Peter Thomas, Senior Herald of the Unicorn Hunters. The Unicorn Hunters also have started Punsters Unlimited, an annual word-banishment list, Lizzie Borden Liberation Day, Snowman Burnings, a World Sauntering Society, and much more. The Sauntering Society, which disdains quick and destination-oriented travel, claims thousands of members. To obtain a questing license and more information about the club's activities, send $1 to Unicorn Hunters, Office of College Relations, Lake Superior State College, Sault Ste. Marie, MI 49783.

During the International Frisbee Contest held near Houghton, teams from across the United States and Canada battle in a spectacular event called Guts Frisbee. Guts Frisbee, which originated in 1958 at tiny Eagle Harbor, pairs five-man teams who face each other at 45 feet. They take turns maniacally whizzing the plastic disk at each other, trying to catch the knuckle-bashing whirr. A crowd usually gathers around to ponder the players' sanity.

Friendly competition isn't confined to the young. In Wakefield, the old-timers are creating a flurry of activity by par-

These women belonged to the Marquette Snowshoe Club.

117

ticipating in the Senior Citizens Olympics. The event includes the usual recreational sports such as bowling and golf, but there's also fly casting, a tall-tale contest, and (here's more compulsive throwing) an egg-tossing contest. One year, to everyone's amazement, a nearly blind woman won the Bocci Ball contest—an Italian game of skill. Unpredictability is normal in the U.P.

There are a variety of wonderful festivals held throughout the Upper Peninsula including the North Country Folk Festival in Ironwood. The U.P. is sometimes accused of being behind the times, but the log cabin builders, weavers, instrument makers, and other crafts people at this festival take that as a compliment. Visitors can also unlimber to Irish jigs and reels, or do some clogging or square-dancing to American tunes, while "The Tamburitzans," a Slavic dance group, teaches a circle dance called the Kolo. Whatever the specialty, these folks are proud to show that old-style skills and ethnic traditions are flourishing.

The specialty promoted in Aura, near L'Anse, is fiddling. At the Fiddler's Jamboree you can wander from small group to group listening to old and young informally trading hand-whacking Irish fiddle tunes such as "The Red-Haired Boy" and "Soldier's Joy." Most of the players are from Michigan, and some play Finnish polkas as well as American fiddle tunes. Other instrumentalists are also in profusion, and with refreshments and good music on tap in this tiny rural area, it's like visiting a room in fiddler's heaven.

After one summer full of these kinds of gatherings, I was careening down a bumpy bush road one typically treacherous snowy November day, the flakes as big as frisbees, when suddenly, three tiny, brightly decorated sports cars roared up behind me. What were *they* doing there? I was just taking a *cruise*—driving randomly in a pointless fashion. But these crazed and determined drivers rumbled throatily past me at the first opportunity. Later I learned that they were members of the Press-On-Regardless Road Rally, the harshest, most challenging and punishing road race in North America. It's held each year on the devious backwoods roads of the Copper Country. Typically only half the cars are able to finish, which explained the ragged creatures huddled around a fire I passed

![decorative divider]

Several members of the cast in a play at the original Skanee Town Hall were local residents. Those who posed here in 1902 included from left: Gust Lundberg, Fred Lundberg, Gertrude Lundberg, Carl Lundberg, and an unidentified play promoter.

photo courtesy of Thomas Oakes

118

later that muddy night. I had thought they were normal, weather-ignoring U.P. folks having a wiener roast.

When the weather turns even colder, and the flakes fall faster, larger, and deeper than Mount St. Helen's ash, snowmobiles come out of summer hibernation. In Sault Ste. Marie, 12,000 stomping spectators gather to watch the I-500 snowmobile race. The snowmobile cowboys thunder around a one-mile oval track at speeds greater than 90 m.p.h. For those interested in more sedate action there are plenty of places to unload the machines. From snowmobiling in Chippewa County's village of Paradise to playing a form of snowmobile poker in Munising, every county has miles of meandering trails to offer.

Groomed cross-county ski trails are also nearly as plentiful as snowflakes, and of course you can always just head off along abandoned logging trails or railroad grades. Dozens of cross-country races are held, with Keweenaw County's Brockway Mountain race one of the most spectacular and challenging. There are great slopes for downhill skiers, and both racing and recreational activities abound. Indianhead Mountain near Wakefield, for example, holds special races that attract both competitors and alert spectators—the Bartenders' Pro-Am Classic and the Bikini Races. The Bartenders' Classic honors the brave servers who must survive the barrage of those who order fiery liquids to fend off the chill of U.P. winters, while the Bikini Races allow women to ski for free if they show up in bikinis.

Obviously, we shovelers and swatters have lots to do besides shoveling and swatting. Fit participants can immerse themselves in a blizzard of games and sports; spectators can observe a swarm of action-packed competitions and festivals. Throughout the marvelous seasons, the Upper Peninsula promises a feast for the senses. Now when you visit the Upper Peninsula and see a car hopelessly stuck in a snowbank, its driver stumbling around in his swimming trunks and yelling, "Driftbusting! Driftbusting!" as he swings a beat-up chain saw in one hand and waves a frisbee in the other, you can nod wisely. Just wave back and smile—in the Upper Peninsula, we call that enjoying oneself!

photo courtesy of Superior View, Marquette

Roller ball was a popular pastime. These men played at the Casino Roller Rink in the 1890s.

photo courtesy of Superior View, Marquette

120

Les Cheneaux—The Snows

Probably no area in the United States can boast a larger concentration of wood-hulled, classic boats than the Les Cheneaux Islands in Michigan's Upper Peninsula. Estimates of the number of old-time, sleek runabouts, canoes, and sailing craft (even a small steamboat,) all of which preceded modern fiberglass and aluminum hulls, reach 400 in this picturesque resort area.

The Les Cheneaux Islands (pronounced Lay-Shen-No and known locally as "The Snows") is a chain of 36 wooded islands stretching along Lake Huron's north shore east of the Mackinac Bridge which shelter a number of calm bays and provide boaters with breathtaking vistas. To demonstrate the boating history of the area, the Les Cheneaux community hosts an antique and classic boat show each August. It is believed to be the largest of its kind in the country and, since its founding in 1978, has become well-known among classic boat owners throughout the East and Midwest. More than 100 boats from small rowing skiffs to sleek, long cabin cruisers line the docks at the small village of Hessel for the annual Les Cheneaux Antique Boat Show. Now sponsored by the Les Cheneaux Historical Association, the show was initiated by summer cottagers Charles Letts, Jr., of Birmingham and Kenneth Horsburgh, of Cleveland, Ohio, and by local boat works owner Jim Mertaugh. About 75 percent of the boats in the show are locally owned, with an increasing number imported each summer from as far away as New York. Antique boating is catching on in part because of shows such as the one at Hessel, which draws attention to the craftsmanship and superior operation of the old wood-hulled vessels. Manufactured since the turn of the century by Chris-Craft, Hacker, Century, Racine Boat Works, Truscott, and other boat builders, many of these gems still exist at Les Cheneaux and, indeed, see everyday utility and pleasure service throughout the summer.

The Les Cheneaux Islands first attracted the attention of visitors in the late 1800s because of the excellent fishing offered in the sheltered bays and channels. Early resorters on Mackinac Island took day-long excursion cruises to the islands on the boats of George Arnold, and caught jumbo perch, bass, pike, and other game fish from the decks of the small steamers.

William A. Patrick, one of Les Cheneaux's first settlers, wanted to accommodate these daytime anglers for longer periods of time and, after arranging with Arnold for such a venture, set up some tents on The Snows Channel in 1887. There were no roads

Early visitors to the Les Cheneaux Islands found excellent fishing grounds. They pitched their tents beside the clear waters and began an ongoing tradition of summer vacations in "The Snows."

then, and not even any docks in the vicinity, so a raft was pushed out from shore to unload visitors from the excursion boats and haul them back to the camp. The following year, Patrick erected a log building to replace the tents. It could sleep only about 26 persons, so adventuresome anglers often overflowed the building and slept in the stables, barns and tents. The excellent fishing made such inconvenience worthwhile, however, and Patrick's Landing, the name still used today, became the area's first resort. But fishing was only one attraction of the area. Northern Michigan's crisp, pollen-free air became a refuge for hay fever victims, and resort areas such as Les Cheneaux were soon claiming relief for countless afflictions of the body and mind. As Cedarville and Hessel established themselves around lumber and commercial fishing, resorters began to arrive sooner each year and stay longer, soon adding a new element to the communities: the cottagers.

Initially from the Bay City area, but later arriving from the industrial centers of Ohio, Illinois, Indiana, and Kentucky, the cottagers at Les Cheneaux sought solitude from other crowded resort areas around the Great Lakes. The cottagers were industrialists, retailers, speculators—largely wealthy and conservative.

The Les Cheneaux Club on Marquette Island was established in 1890, and the millionaires who colonized the island with summer mansions dedicated themselves to preserving the area's natural beauty. Other islands similarly developed, and today Government Island is the only island not privately owned.

To accommodate the needs of the cottagers, local residents began to turn to new trades. The late Guy Hamel, son of a local commercial fisherman, carved out a successful career in real estate and became the chief guide, developer, and promoter of the area until his death in the late 1970s. Hamel would brag that he never owned a car, and that he sold practically all of his real estate by boat.

Other local residents became builders of fine boats to supply the tourist and resort fishing businesses and to provide early cottagers with transportation to their island cottages. Bruce Patrick, grandson of William, began building boats around 1930 when he was 15. Even before then, he recalls, each summer season was marked with Fourth of July boat races that would challenge the best

of the locally-made craft. Each year, boat builders such as Joe Cramin, Ross Patrick, Louis Folmer, George Dunn, and Robert and Harrison Hamel would secretly develop their latest entry. Nobody knew what the competition would produce at the race, and there were no limits to the size and power of the craft. The annual races subsequently became more organized and included different classes for speedboats, sailboats, outboards, rowboats, and canoes. The races were replaced in the early 1960s by "watercades" in which boats would parade through the channels and around the islands. Today, the big attraction is the annual boat show. But, while the activities have changed, the boats remain the same.

Probably the largest influence on wooden boat activity in the Les Cheneaux Islands today is E.J. Mertaugh's Boat Works at Hessel which, in 1926, bcame the world's first franchised Chris-Craft dealer. Founder Gene Mertaugh held the exclusive territory from Bay City to Ontario. "I sold all the boats in The Snows," Mertaugh says of those early years. He recalls that Chris-Craft boats became popular after World War I. Their design and use of surplus aircraft engines (the Curtis OX5) allowed them to travel up to 30 miles per hour—far more attractive than the 20 miles per hour most other boats could reach at that time.

Gene Mertaugh believes Les Cheneaux, itself, is probably the greatest factor that allowed so many of those early boats to survive the years. The cool water, sheltered bays, and short summer season helped preserve the wood hulls, making it easier for the owners to keep their boats in tiptop shape. In earlier days, Mertaugh remembers, complete restoration of a boat, including replacement of deteriorated planking, upholstery, and the many coats of varnish required would cost the owner about $1,000. That cost today runs closer to $7,000 or $8,000, but it's worth the money when the result may be a $20,000 boat. In fact, the maintenance required for a wooden boat, Mertaugh contends, is worth the time and money to those who appreciate its responsiveness to the elements. Nothing, he says, outperforms a well-made wood hull in the water.

The sight of so many of these classic boats at the Les Cheneaux Antique Boat Show recalls a time of fine craftsmanship and design, and an appreciation of boating that has never left the area.

This old postcard depicts the famous Islington fishing grounds in the Les Cheneaux Islands.

photo by Superior View, Marquette

Upper Crust Camps

Few areas of the United States are endowed with such a rugged, real wilderness atmosphere and are still so close to population centers as Michigan's Upper Peninsula. To many, the peninsula has the curiosity and flavor of a foreign land. It is a place where not only millions of tourists *pass through,* but where many come to *stay*—for weeks, months, and even the whole summer. Many vacationers return several times in the same year, or come back year after year to the same place. And there are those who love the land so much that they buy or build vacation homes here. Below the Straits these are called cottages. Here they are called camps. Because many of the owners are absent for much of the year, they meet with various types of problems and may get a local partner, or join with several absentee partners to better utilize and maintain the camp. When the partnership involves more than four or five, it might evolve into a club, and through combined efforts, the maintenance expenses and responsibilities can be divided equally.

There are thousands of these camps, partnerships, and clubs across the Upper Peninsula. One of the oldest and most respected is the Huron Mountain Club on the shores of Lake Superior in Marquette County. Established in 1889, it developed its own tradition of respected conservation policies. Another club in the east end of the peninsula nearly as old is the Les Cheneaux Island Club or the "Snows" as it is often referred to. South of Ishpeming is the Northwoods Club, somewhat younger but still considered an old and well established organization. The Hiawatha Club, east of Manistique, is the largest of its type in the Upper Peninsula, both in membership and the amount of land ownership. Some of the later clubs, such as the Four Island Lake Association (FILA) north of Champion, bought their land intact, but most started with a forty or two and added to their holdings as land became available. Because many of the camps were formed shortly after the logging companies swept through the U.P., much of the land was inexpensive and in a rather sorry state. The owners had only to build a few rustic log buildings, let trees grow in the logging roads—thereby making the land less accessible—and sit back to watch the acreage become a priceless paradise of flora and fauna.

Some camps were private estates which became too expensive to be maintained by individuals, and eventually fell into the hands of the state or federal government. Such examples of this are Craig Lake State Park in Baraga County, and the Fisher Estate (Fisher

The tepee at left is one of the many unique fireplaces at Granot Loma. George Kaufman, builder of the camp, was very proud of his one-quarter Indian blood and furnished the magnificent home with Indian artifacts, paintings, and Navajo rugs.

photo courtesy of Superior View, Marquette

Body Company) in Gogebic County, which is now a national park known as the Sylvania Tract.

One of the finest camps in the Upper Peninsula is Granot Loma, located in Marquette County. Its builder, Louis G. Kaufman, was not an outsider nor a wealthy industrialist from a far-off city but an Upper Peninsula native, born and reared in Marquette. Mr. Kauffman left the U.P. during the winter to make his mark on the world, but he spent practically all of his adult summers at his camp on the shores of Lake Superior. Built just after World War I, Granot Loma is a tribute to local craftmanship. It demonstrates one area where it's hard to beat U.P. craftspeople—logworking. There are scores of good examples across the peninsula. Granot Loma is perched on a sandstone ledge with a steel and 10-foot-thick cement foundation all faced with native rock. From there up, the structure is log. The main sitting room is 120 feet long, 60 feet wide, and 40 feet high. There are 60 fireplaces throughout, including one in the main hall that will take six-foot logs. It even has room for a person or two to sit on a stone bench and drink a morning cup of coffee, as Mrs. Kaufman was accustomed to doing. Another fireplace is shaped like a tepee, and still another has a window above it, causing some wonder as to where the smoke goes.

There is an Indian motif throughout the approximately seventy rooms as Mr. Kaufman was very proud of his one-quarter Indian blood. Everywhere there are priceless woodcarvings and paintings—many of which portray famous Indian chiefs—and the plank floors are covered with huge Navajo rugs. There are rooms finished in cobblestone, birch bark, cedar bark, and local woods all cleverly fitted to make a most pleasing effect. At one time the massive basement held a complete maintenance shop and a dozen or so boats and canoes of various sizes. It also housed a motor-powered tram to bring the boats to the breakwater-enclosed harbor. In its heyday, Granot Loma required a staff of more than two

Rustic elegance and comfort characterized many of the camps such as this one at the Huron Mountain Club.

126

photo courtesy of Marquette County Historical Society

dozen to keep the whole estate running smoothly. Kaufman died in 1942, and the lodge and surrounding lands are now owned by a son-in-law, Jack Martin.

Henry Ford's cabin, twenty miles or so up the shore, is another marvel. It is constructed of huge hand-hewn white pine logs, and has porches crafted from the native slate gathered at a quarry in nearby Baraga County. This was Ford's Upper Peninsula home for the month of August during the last 18 years of his life.

The oldest and possibly grandest of all the secluded private estates in Michigan's Upper Peninsula belonged to Cyrus H. McCormick of Chicago, son of the inventor and builder of most of the early agricultural implements used on American farms for half a century. The lakes, rivers, timber, waterfalls, and the inaccessability of the western end of the Upper Peninsula made it unsurpassed as a wilderness retreat. Cyrus McCormick first came to the U.P. in 1885, accompanied by naturalist William C. Gray, one of McCormick's professors at Princeton University. Gray had selected the area because it held the origin of several rivers—all flowing in different directions. It is the second highest spot in Michigan, and it has an abundance of fresh water, wildlife, and rugged beauty.

The year before his exploration of the U.P. with Gray, McCormick's father had died. Young Cyrus was only 26 years old at the time and, although he inherited the presidency of the company, his mother took over running it with help from her brother and they sent young Cyrus off on the camping trip.

He fell in love with the area and returned whenever possible throughout the rest of his life. At first, he stayed on lumber company land, and later purchased 160 acres on Fortress Lake, which he named. His acreage included an island on which he set up his summer campsite. It was to this summer tent camp that he returned frequently while still a young man, hiring local guides and woodsmen to set it up each year and act as caretakers.

Henry Ford spent many summers at this camp which he built at the Huron Mountain Club.

photo by Koehne

Around the turn of the century, a "harvester war" developed, with fifteen or more companies making farm equipment and trying to undersell each other. McCormick Farm Machinery was the oldest and largest company, and when financier J. P. Morgan suggested an amalgamation of the companies—even coining the name International Harvester—McCormick was skeptical. Concerned that his company's business could only be hurt, and that the legal problems of such a merger would be insurmountable, he hired the most vigorous attorney he knew to represent him, a Chicagoan about his age named Cyrus Bentley.

For a year or so during the negotiations, McCormick could hardly speak without first asking Bentley for permission. They became fast friends and were soon off on a camping trip to McCormick's favorite part of the world. Bentley was ecstatic with the beautiful wilderness. He couldn't get enough of it. The two men made plans to become partners in an Upper Peninsula venture. They wanted to build a permanent camp there, and also to become members of the Huron Mountain Club, 25 miles to the north where both had friends already established.

In 1902 the International Harvester Company was formed, and that same year McCormick and Bentley went together to the island camp at Fortress Lake. They hired workers to build a cabin on the mainland, and they took options on surrounding land so that they could purchase it when the lumbermen were finished with it. Bentley liked the idea of hiking cross-country the 25 or 30 miles north through relatively virgin country to Huron Mountain.

A few years later, after carefully examining all the lakes and rivers close by, they decided that McCormick's original campsite on the island was most suitable for building. A men's camp and a women's camp were the first to be constructed. In 1905 and 1906, Bentley and McCormick built a large double lodge to house both of

Cyrus Bentley, above, was hired by Cyrus McCormick to represent the McCormick Farm Machinery company. The two men became close friends, and eventually developed a partnership which included the purchase of a large parcel of land in the Upper Peninsula and establishment of a permanent camp there. The view at right of Cyrus McCormick on the trail between his camp and the Huron Mountain Club was taken from a 1905 stereo view.

photo courtesy of Fred Rydholm

their families, thus circumventing the problems of who would get the best spot, who would build first, and who had the best cabin.

Both the foundation and chimney of the structure were made of native stones. The building was divided through the middle by a wall, and one side could not be reached from the other without first going outside to one of the porches. Each family furnished their own side, and the lodge was so complete that either family could live independently of the other. The men admitted that the best moments of their lives were spent there, in their own private wilderness. When they were hard at work in the busy financial world, thoughts of their cabin in the far north kept them cheerful.

Mrs. Bentley didn't take to the rugged wilderness camp life quite as enthusiastically as did her husband. She preferred the more social life at the Huron Mountain Club, so her family built a second cabin for her there. For the next twenty years, Bentley spent his leisure hours planning, hiking, and improving the trail he had built between the two places. The McCormicks and Bentleys went to their Fortress Lake retreat as often as they could throughout the spring, summer, and fall. In addition, one family had the cabin all to themselves in July, the other in August.

In 1908, woodsman Ed McLean spotted an albino deer in the area. The animal appeared many times over the next few years, much to the delight of guests, and Fortress Lake was renamed Whitedeer Lake. The name is appropriate even today. There seems to be a tendency to albinism among deer in Marquette and Baraga Counties and many have been seen since then.

Bentley relocated his trail in 1914 and 1915. The new trail was superior in every respect except that it was slightly longer, so he built a halfway cabin in the wilderness between Whitedeer Lake and Huron Mountain. This added greatly to the pleasure and excitement of the trail, and Bentley found himself spending much time at the

photo by George Shiras, III

After woodsman Ed McLean spotted an albino deer at the Bentley-McCormick estate, Fortress Lake was renamed Whitedeer Lake, the name it retains today. This view of an albino buck was taken by wildlife photographer George Shiras III about 1915.

photo courtesy of Fred Rydholm

far-off trail cabin he called "Arbutus Lodge."

While Cyrus Bentley worked on his trails, McCormick's project was to locate a huge glacial boulder—there were many on the property—and have it moved to the family cemetery plot at Graceland Cemetery in Chicago. McCormick selected a 24-ton rock and had it covered with damp burlap to protect the lichens and tiny oak ferns which grew on it. Then it was carefully crated and mounted on a skid. With one of the very early International Harvester tractors it was dragged down the 16-mile road to Champion. Each of the nine abandoned railroad bridges that crossed and recrossed the Peshekee River had to be shored up with temporary pilings to withstand the weight. At Champion, the rock was placed on a flatcar and taken to Chicago on the Chicago & Northwestern Railroad. The ferns and lichens died in their new environment, but today the rock sits half submerged in the McCormick burial plot in Graceland Cemetery so that the family, even in death, may be near their Shangri-la.

McCormick's wife died on January 17, 1921. A year later, Cyrus married his secretary—much to the chagrin of Bentley and other friends and employees. Preferring to spend time on their own property, McCormick and his new wife dropped their Huron Mountain membership, and the decades-long McCormick-Bentley partnership began to falter. In 1927, the two families permanently went separate ways. The McCormicks took over the entire Whitedeer Lake property and the Bentleys moved to Huron Mountain. Cyrus Bentley died in 1931 but his grandchildren and great-grandchildren continue to return there.

Harold McCormick, a younger brother of Cyrus, married Edith Rockefeller, daughter of John D. Rockefeller. They continued to use the property on occasion, as did many of their friends, business associates, and employees of the McCormick estate. Cyrus died in 1938, leaving Whitedeer Lake Camp to his second son, Gor-

Bentley built a new trail to the Huron Mountain Club in 1914 and 1915. It was longer than the first trail, so he built a halfway cabin called Arbutus Lodge, shown here during construction.

130

photo courtesy of Fred Rydholm

don, an architect and bachelor. Gordon kept a full-time maintenance crew there under the watchful eye of camp superintendent Ted Tonkin, whose tenure went back to the early Bentley-and-McCormick days. In the 1940s, Gordon made many elaborate improvements to the area, but an attempt to reopen the trails failed. He also hired expert logworker Nilo Kallioinen from the Rolling Mill Location south of Negaunee.

Kallioinen was a true craftsman. He had worked on Granot Loma as a young man, and was head carpenter at the Sam Cohodas Lodge on Lake Michigamme in 1936. Gordon designed several projects for Kallioinen to build including an $80,000 boathouse, a $50,000 woodshed, bridges, furniture, and curiosities. The craftsman's abilities amazed Gordon, who offered to bring Kallioinen to Chicago and set him up in a shop. But Kallioinen was not interested in leaving the Upper Peninsula. In 1948, he undertook a major renovation of the Chimney cabin, first building a new roof high above the old one, completely enclosing it, then reconstructing the whole cabin inside. The walls were made several logs higher and a second porch was added.

Although he continued to maintain a year-round crew, Gordon McCormick never returned to Whitedeer Lake after 1947 because of health problems. Before his death in 1967, he made arrangements to leave the accumulated 17,000 acres to the United States Government in care of the U.S. Forest Service for experimental use. He hoped that the land would forever remain the wilderness his family loved so much. Since the Forest Service took over in 1969, many experimental projects and studies involving the land, animals, plants, and people have taken place there with little disturbance to the grounds. The buildings, however, are deteriorating from disuse. The thousands of undeveloped acres remain a tribute to the efforts and dreams of Cyrus McCormick and Cyrus Bentley. Theirs truly was the ultimate in private camps.

Cyrus McCormick left Whitedeer Lake Camp to his son Gordon, pictured above. Gordon made many improvements to the estate and hired a full-time maintenance crew to care for it. He left the 17,000 acre compound to the United States government in care of the U.S. Forest Service, which took it over in 1969.

photo courtesy of Marquette County Historical Society, Marquette

132

Agricultural Oddities

Although Michigan's Upper Peninsula lies within a well-defined hay-dairy-potatoes agricultural region, the U.P.'s history includes some peculiar land use gambits. In the past century, commercial volumes of cranberries, celery, peanuts, ginseng, peppermint and blueberries have rooted, blossomed, and withered as potentially redemptive crops for the area's intractable topography.

The first stage of agricultural development in the Upper Peninsula reflected a cooperation between resident Indians and the white settlers. The Chippewa, Ottawa, and Potawatomi became the U.P.'s first serious gardeners after their initial contact with early 17th Century settlers. Jesuits at Sault Ste. Marie cleared land for wheat which they planted and harvested with Indian aid; and the Indians helped missionary and military settlements garden, while independently gathering potatoes, peas, corn, and wild rice to trade with the whites. Methodist missionary John H. Pitezel was active in the U.P. from 1843 to 1857 and noted several instances of farming hay, potatoes, and turnips by both the Indians and missionaries.

The mining boom spurred the next stage of U.P. agriculture. Immigrant miners in the Copper Country and the iron ranges created a large market for local produce, livestock, and dairy products. Dissatisfied miners, especially the Finns, supplied the raw, relentless labor necessary to clear the land and start small farms. The U.P. has always been at least 80 percent forested, and many early farms were "40-acre stump ranches," made amenable to plow and pasture by men who saw such backbreaking work as their only hope for freedom from the mines. The lumber boom that followed the mining boom produced thousands of acres of similar land for sale; and the U.P.'s agricultural peak followed the lumber and mining crests by the two decades needed to clear the cutover. Agricultural acreage reached 465,000 in 1919.

It has only been in the last century that people have looked closely at much of this peninsula's land, wondered what on earth to do with it, and resorted to the odd crops mentioned above. But their paths to success were strewn with pebbles (among other hurdles.)

What this glacially raked peninsula grows best is wood and rock. Precambrian outcrop dominates the west half; sand and muck glacial lake beds—lyrically labeled "open wet savannas" by landlooker John Munro Longyear—lie across the east. Gravelly moraines suture the rock, peat and sand together. A short growing season (the 90 days of June, July and August, although killing

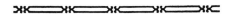

It took only three seeds to produce this fine selection of crops grown on pine barrens at the Haight Farm.

MAKE A DELICIOUS HOMEMADE HUCKLEBERRY PIE

Recipe

Mix berries and juice with 3 tablespoons of corn starch, fill pie shell with mixture, cover with top crust which has several cuts to allow steam to escape. Bake at 400 degrees F. for 30 minutes.

THIS CAN OF BERRIES WILL MAKE A 9 INCH PIE

label courtesy of Ted Bays, Marquette

frosts sometimes occur in these months too) and a long haul to the major Midwest markets compound the basic obstacle of 80 percent forestation. This adamant terrain acquired an additional impediment to agriculture during the lumbering era, when thousands of acres of pine cutover were left denuded of the one crop they best sustained. And much of the land passed via tax delinquency from the hands of distant, disinterested corporation owners into state ownership. State and federal forest is obviously most likely to be managed for wood products, not farm crops. But a few adventurous, diligent, foolish, visionary and occasionally successful souls overcame these obstacles and found unusual uses for the land.

State geologist Frank Leverett's thorough 1911 soil survey showed something which Michigan Indians and trappers had known for centuries: Unlike the vast pine plains of the Lower Peninsula, Michigan's Upper Peninsula is riddled with large potholes, swales and bogs of peat and muck soil. The reflex response of industrial society to damp land seems to be, emphatically, *drainage,* and that was Leverett's recommendation. But some of the leatherleaf and sphagnum moss harbored its own clue to profitable use of the bog lands. Early Michigan explorers, and the Indians, found an abundance of cranberries growing along marshy shore lands. The acidic soils provided the nutrients required by the plant, and the temperate lakeshore provided the protection against frost necessary in this unpredictable latitude. In 1876 at Whitefish Point, a location west of the Soo on Lake Superior more noted for shipwrecks and fishing, two determined men put the native cranberry to commercial use.

Canadian traveler John Clarke and Scottish sea captain Alex Barclay spent the winter of 1874 at Whitefish Point in a sod house. They enlisted the aid of Clarke's half-brother Frank E. House, and by 1876 they began tending a commercial cranberry bog of stock

134

refined from the native local plants. The low promontory of land allowed easy flooding from a ditch-and-dike system to prevent frosty nights from killing the berries. From 1890 to 1910, Whitefish Point and nearby Vermilion shipped 400-500 bushels annually via packet schooner to Midwest holiday dinner tables.

But cranberries don't usually grow well in the same place forever. Natural plant succession of an evolving biota created the bogs, and natural succession killed them. The relentless incursion of tag alder eventually smothered the cranberries on Whitefish Point.

A variety of vegetables were thriving downstate near Grand Rapids in a type of soil similar to the Upper Peninsula muck. The Old World crop, celery, grew particularly well, and was finding new favor as a delicacy in America. The Golden Plume variety which had been subject to blight in other areas grew heartily in a 2½-acre trial plot on the east side of Newberry, just down a dirt road from the Detroit, Mackinac & Marquette railroad depot. By 1888, two celery farms had expanded that acreage tenfold. The obvious rail connections via the DM&M enabled independent celery grower James G. Van Tuyl to market his crops easily. "Newberry Celery Served Here" proclaimed many U.P. hotel menus. Van Tuyl's O. K. Celery Gardens spread Newberry's identity as The Celery City throughout Michigan and the Midwest. In 1927, competition from the newer, hardier Pascal variety of celery, grown by southern farmers with better marketing opportunities and a longer growing season, edged out the Newberry crop.

That same year, another Lower Peninsula muck-land crop sprouted in a U.P. peat bog. Peppermint harvested from 25 acres of mid-Schoolcraft County peat soil was sold to Wrigley Bros. in Chicago for about $30 per pound. The mint farm was designed by University of Wisconsin professor Harold Stewart, and it served as a

Northern Canneries operated at Newberry, an area that was also the site of James G. Van Tuyl's famous celery gardens.

photo courtesy of Janice Gerred, Lansing

photo courtesy of Janice Gerred, Lansing

demonstrational unit for Marquette University and its multi-talented, visionary business manager Henry L. Banzhaf. The purpose was to show the value of some of the university's 250,000 Upper Peninsula acres—acquired through default on investment bonds by the Northern Michigan Land Co. Although the farm also included varieties of locally popular crops such as hay, rye, and potatoes, the mint crops undoubtedly imitated the great mint industry of southern Michigan and northern Indiana. Stewart probably knew that 90 percent of the world's supply of mint oil came from within a 90 mile radius of Kalamazoo. And he surely knew, when the mint farm was planted in 1926, that a frost had destroyed the 1925 Michigan and Indiana crop, rocketing prices from $4 to $30 per pound.

By 1929, Stewart's farm had expanded to 78 acres; but so had many other mint farms. Prices had already dropped back to $4 per pound by the summer of 1926, and it was only because of three-year buying agreements that many farmers were able to stay in business until 1929. Then they quit minting; and that year, so did Marquette University. Eventually, the university's U.P. land holdings reverted to the state for tax delinquencies, and The Northern Michigan Land Company, then, turned the only real profit on the mint farm land by unloading some pine cutover as surety on defaulted bonds.

Not all lumber companies did so well with cutover, although some dealt through front companies in the Upper Peninsula Development Bureau to sell their timberland to farmers. Cleveland-Cliffs Iron Co., among others, volunteered 1 cent per acre on their holdings to support the Development Bureau. In the 1920s, U.P. newspapers were thick with the Bureau's lush prose touting the virtues of "Cloverland"—that pastoral euphemism for the Upper Peninsula based on the false notion that pine cutover grew back in clover, a forage ideal for dairy cattle and sheep. The Duluth, South Shore & Atlantic railroad (descendant of Peter White's DM&M) advertised "meadowlands" for sale, but that poetic description of swamp and cutover was as licentious as Longyear's "savannas."

During the early decades of this century, advertisements and potential sales of such land sprouted everywhere. In 1911, the Northern Michigan Land Company offered 250,000 acres in the Tahquamenon Valley and near Seney, and proposed blasting the Tahquamenon Falls to drain some of the surrounding swamp. A St. Paul land syndicate almost bought most of the Tahquemenon River

From 1890 to 1910, Whitefish Point and nearby Vermilion shipped 400 to 500 bushels of cranberries annually. Most of the berries made their way to Midwest holiday dinner tables, but some went into cranberry jelly as the label above indicates. These workers at the Frank House Farm, top right, paused from washing cranberries just long enough to let a photographer take their picture.

photo courtesy of Memorial Library Archives of Marquette University Milwaukee, Wisconsin

flats, and a Wisconsin firm scouted Schoolcraft County swamp for moss harvestable as a fiber base for carpeting. The U.P. Development Bureau propaganda attested to the U.P.'s annual production of two crops of clover, and described the Bureau's fattening demonstrational cattle herd to substantiate that testimony.

But again, the best crop for pine cutover grew right under the developers' feet—if they ever actually walked the land they promoted—and the Indians had been using it for centuries. Cutover grows back in blueberries. Along railroad lines, settlers and Indians had been picking berries and selling them for transshipment to the south in commercial volume from Ishpeming and Negaunee since the 1870s. The Peter White Corporation built a cannery in Marquette's lower harbor in 1914, planning to send boats of pickers along the lakeshore to augment the railroad picking. They never canned a quart. But when the Depression supplied cheap labor, blueberries in commercial volume did roll out of several U.P. cities.

The biggest dealers in blueberries were John Beechler of the Soo, and the Michigan Blueberry Co. of Newberry, formed by DSS&A freight agent Bill Nichols and Newberry grocer Joe Rahilly. In late July, carloads of migrant pickers from across the country would surge into the blueberry plains. In 1931, more than 1500 people were scouring Luce County for berries, and encampments in Alger, Schoolcraft, Mackinac and Chippewa counties added to the area's $500,000 blueberry harvest. At $1.60 per case, a family of good pickers could earn $8 to $10 per day—attractive wages in the Depression. Brokers daily shipped 500 to 700 crates of untreated or sugar-packed berries to every state in the union.

Local residents joined in the berry bonanza. John Singleton, whose father was lighthouse keeper at Crisp Point for years, picked berries and sold them to Rahilly to earn money for school clothes. Singleton remembers the large camp at Uhls near the East Branch of the Two Hearted River, where the pickers would string lanterns and hold dances on the bridge at night. Beda Erickson picked for John Beechler at his blueberry picking camp on the Danaher Plains. Her father, Charles, hauled the berries by horse-drawn wagon to the DSS&A siding at Danaher for shipment.

Eventually, the abundant supply of blueberries fostered a small cannery near Newberry. Ernest Troop, a periodic vistor to the area, began hauling truckloads of berries back down to his St. Johns

This tractor was used to break up peat on the well-known Mint Farm in Schoolcraft County.

137

home. In 1945, Troop built a cannery on Spring Hill, about four miles north of Newberry. The operation used 100 cases of berries a day, for which Troop paid pickers $5 per case. The Troops hauled their berries downstate, and brought peaches and cherries back to can at Newberry. They also canned some commodities for the Newberry State Hospital, from the hospital gardens. The cannery lacked sufficient berries in the early 1950s to operate profitably, and ceased operations by 1955.

Forests, like bogs, do not stand still. They evolve within the limits defined by soil and climate. And pine plains evolve from blueberries and related scrub bushes to aspen and jack pine. Eventually forest fire control and ecological succession reduced blueberries from steady commercial to merely local occasional volume. Cranberries, blueberries, mint—all were native, seasonal crops that commanded a relatively high price per volume. Peanuts, however, fit none of those categories and proved several rules by its failure.

Sam Crawford, successor to Jesse Spalding's lumber holdings along the Cedar River in 1899, expected his first peanut crop to be a huge success. The thick agricultural handbook he carried said peanuts would grow anywhere potatoes did. So in the summer of 1913, Crawford's farm manager, Joe Rouleau, and his sons cleared about five acres along the forest trail south of the Cedar River company store where, among other items sold to woods workers in the area, peanuts always did a brisk trade. The next summer, Rouleau broadcast the seed, stuck in some artichokes between the peanut hills, and waited. But when he saw the meager goobers that nudged through the soil that summer, and when he tasted them, Rouleau didn't wait long to determine the crop's fate. Hogs from a nearby company farm quickly snuffed out and consumed the U.P.'s oddest, shortest agricultural experiment. The artichokes, rooting like quackgrass, lingered until about 1916. Three miles south of Cedar River in Menominee County, on the west side of M-35 where it bends away from Lake Michigan, a small clearing bristling with insurgent aspen is still known as the Peanut Farm. Like the Mint Farm, this brief, doomed adventure has succeeded in local place-name lore.

Not all agriculture in Menominee County fared so poorly. One specialty crop, ginseng, capitilized on the rich soil and lumbering's

The success of James Van Tuyl's OK Celery Gardens spread Newberry's fame throughout the Midwest as the "Celery City."

photo courtesy of Marquette County Historical Society, Marquette

138

detritus. Cedar tops filtered sunlight into ginseng arbors, constructed of the scrap and lath from local lumber mills. The oriental market for ginseng demanded scrupulous weeding to bring in a pure product, so a mere one-acre arbor occupied all of one farmer's time. When picked, the roots had to be dried in 110-degree heat, often obtained by stoking kitchen stoves until the attic—and the rest of the house—became unbearably hot.

The big payoff for careful tending came in 1927-29, when ginseng sold for $38.50 per pound, a nice improvement over the $18 paid since the crop's inception in Menominee County in 1908. The root's financial magic vanished for Menominee growers in 1931, however, when internal China politics and the Japanese invasion closed many trade routes. The plunge in prices forced one Stephenson farmer to sell a $25,000 crop for $1,200.

The Upper Peninsula's odd crops carry epilogues of decline and extinction, halting resurrection, tentative experimentation, wild avatars. Blueberries still grow up here, especially where a forest fire has eluded the increasingly tight surveillance of state and federal fire fighters. An agent of the Pet-Ritz Co., looking for pie filling, offered corporate support for redevelopment of the U.P.'s commercial blueberry crop; but when that man died, the project folded. Cranberries still linger at Whitefish Point, but not in the grand volume of the 1890s. Wisconsin's Eagle River Cranberry Co. almost took over a demonstrational cranberry bog developed near Newberry by MSU Extension agent Ray Gummerson in the 1960s, but a federal marketing order throttled that plan. Newberry's Jim Lone, grandson of James Van Tuyl, still tills about 20 acres of the Newberry muck-land his grandfather pioneered 100 years ago. He includes celery among his dozen-odd crops, but he readily admits he makes as much from other ventures as he does from gardening.

That leaves peppermint. There is none on the Mint Farm. The level field that in 1929 grew 78 acres of high-quality mint now sports only dewberry and scrub grass. Not even pioneer species of trees have rooted on the once lush peat soil. But on the wet margins of Indian Lake and other Upper Peninsula lowlands, wild mint still thrives as an aromatic reminder of past attempts to bring those reluctant northern bogs into production.

photo courtesy of Alger County Historical Society

In 1920, these farmers participated in a plowing demonstration at the Upper Peninsula Experimental State Farm in Chatham.

139

photo by Richard Frear, courtesy of National Park Service

Isle Royale

Isle Royale is a wilderness of rocky ridges separated by deep harbors, lakes, and swamps, and surrounded by the clear waters of Lake Superior. The story of its becoming American soil is sometimes attributed to a series of folktales that center around Benjamin Franklin. It is said that Franklin, having read Jesuit missionary writings about copper deposits around Lake Superior, schemed to get Isle Royale in a variety of ways at the 1783 Treaty of Paris. He was supposed to have gotten the British drunk, played poker with them to determine the location of the borderline, or just plain outwitted them. In reality, the island's location floated on maps during the 16th and 17th Centuries because of inaccurate mapping techniques. The map used in the negotiations showed Isle Royale and a second large, mysterious island as being south of their actual location. The borderline description read, *"Thence through Lake Superior northward of the Isles Royal and Phelippeaux."*

The missionary papers that Franklin might have read were reports of Ojibwa Indian stories and explorers' accounts of copper deposits on Isle Royale. The Ojibwa called the island *Minong* meaning, most accurately, a good place to be. But the word is also translated to mean blueberry island, island made of copper, or the disappearing island. The Ojibwa were late comers to the region, and probably had little connection to the more than 4,500-year-old prehistoric copper mine workings. The early explorers described finding shallow pits with hammerstones—made of beach cobbles—strewn in and around the pits. These hammerstones were used to bang away at the rock, following copper veins in the hard basalt, or to open up circular cavities in amygdaloid formations. The prehistoric miners used the copper to make awls, beads, fish hooks, and other objects by pounding or cold hammering the pieces of metal into the desired shape. As on the Keweenaw Peninsula, the prehistoric mine pits on Isle Royale were used by European miners as clues to finding copper in the 1800s. At the Minong Mine, near McCargoe's Cove, miners uncovered hundreds of prehistoric pits as well as large mass copper pieces whose sharp edges had been removed by the prehistoric miners with their hammerstones.

Little evidence has been found of habitation, or of the cultural traits of the prehistoric miners. Ojibwa tales and archeological finds are all that remain.

In 1800, the Northwest Company began fishing the waters of Isle Royale, using the Indians' knowledge and methods. As trading

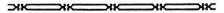

Rocky cliffs and deep blue harbors typify the wilderness beauty of Isle Royale.

photo courtesy of the National Park Service

companies began diversifying, both the Northwest Company and the American Fur Company used Indian and French workers for commercial fishing around the island. In the 1840s, the Jesuit stories about Isle Royale copper enticed many Cornish and Irish miners to the island, and mining exploration began there even before the Ojibwa had deeded the land to the United States. An 1842 treaty signed at LaPointe had failed to include the Grand Portage band of Ojibwa Indians, and it was not until two years later that the U.S. government negotiated a settlement with the Indians for purchase of the island. Once the land was U.S. property, mining claims began in earnest. This first copper boom on the island continued until 1855 when the last of the initial operations closed down. For miners, the island was not a romantic wilderness but an island purgatory which they endured just to make a living. Cornelius G. Shaw's diary of his life at the Smithwick Mine in 1847 describes some of the hardships that threatened his comfort and safety such as insects, cold weather, misfired black powder, broken tools, irregular supply boats, arguments between workers of different nationalities, slow progress, and small production. The unrealized hope for great copper production was discouraging.

During the 1870s, a second attempt to recover the island's copper was made by trained engineers and geologists, and new technology—the diamond drill. Transportation was more reliable by then, and island residents represented several nationalities in a mix similar to mining towns on the mainland.

Isle Royale was declared a county, and the town of Island Mine was designated as the county seat. Much of the money for exploration came from the Quincy Mining Company of Hancock. But the expense and hazards of island life did not balance off against the low production. By 1880, island mining had ceased again.

The last attempts to find copper were centered around the Wendigo Mine during the 1890s. Two years of systematic diamond drill exploration along with trenching determined that there was not

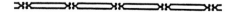

Because of inaccurate mapping techniques, this 1824 map shows Isle Royale and the mysterious Phelippeaux Island as being much larger, and closer to the Upper Peninsula, than they actually are. The lighthouse, above right, stands guard at Menagerie Island.

142

photo by R. Janke, courtesy of National Park Service

enough copper on Isle Royale to make the efforts worthwhile. In 1892, the Isle Royale Land Corporation began to sell off its Wendigo Mine holdings to individuals for summer homes and resorts.

Commercial fishing companies found that they could rent out cabins and services to the tourists who began flocking to the island on excursion boats. By 1902, there were five resorts on the island and newspapers touted Isle Royale as the Mackinac of Lake Superior—the Mecca of fashionable throngs.

The resorts did well. Visitors found the island to be an excellent vacation spot, a hay-fever-free haven with superb fishing and natural beauty. Parcels of land were purchased and summer homes were built. But by the 1920s, a movement to protect the island from further tourism began. The first steps toward making the area Isle Royale National Park were underway.

The island's commercial fishing industry had increased substantially when an extension of the railroad to Duluth included refrigerator cars that could successfully carry the trout, whitefish, and herring to major markets in the Midwest. When the Scandinavians came to Isle Royale, they found the climate and natural setting to be much like their homeland, and many stayed year-round. Small family fishing settlements grew around the island until the 1930s, when a combination of depressed fish prices and the island's national park status began to curtail operations.

Isle Royale had been considered an excellent research site, and its scientific significance helped to support the protection movement. By 1931, the park was established and a ten-year period of land acquisition began. To prepare the island for visitors, the Civilian Conservation Corps worked from 1935 to 1940 to construct trails, docks, and outbuildings. The park was dedicated in 1946, and although it was always considered a wilderness, it was officially dedicated as such in 1976. Today, Isle Royale appears much the same as it did decades ago, and it remains as the Ojibwa first named it, *Minong, a good place to be.*

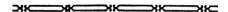

While the early morning mist rises, a lone canoeist glides across Brady's Cove.

photo courtesy of Ontonagon County Historical Museum

The Great Ontonagon Fire

I was pushing logs on the bull chain at the Diamond Match Company's big mill. My wages was 75 cents for a ten-hour day and when my paycheck came around at the end of the month, I had $19.25. Anyway, that morning, I got up and went to work at seven o'clock. It was hot and sultry. The sun was all covered over with haze, just a little ball of fire, and the wind was terrific. Little did we think that by the time the sun went down that night, we'd all be homeless and what we wore would be our only possessions.

O. E. "Del" Woodbury was 16 years old the summer of 1896 when the great fire destroyed Ontonagon. More than 73 years later he recalled the events of that day for me and for members of the Ontonagon County Historical Society.

As early as 1766, before there was a town, visitors and explorers came to the area to see the famous Ontonagon Boulder. Where there was one large chunk of copper, people reasoned, there ought to be more. Indeed, many mines were subsequently built in Ontonagon country which produced vast quantities of solid copper and silver, and ores of varying copper and silver content. Hundreds of companies have mined the area since James K. Paul founded the town and sold the famous boulder in 1843.

The young town of Ontonagon grew rapidly as copper prices rose during the Civil War. After the war, increased use of the telephone, the telegraph, and electricity increased the demand for copper, and mine owners again prospered. Ontonagon eventually acquired wagon roads and railroads, county government, and even law and order.

As the logging business began to dwindle in the Lower Peninsula, lumberjacks swarmed across the Straits and began cutting their way westward across the Upper Peninsula. By 1896, Ontonagon had become a thriving community of 2,300 residents and boasted large and plush hotels, churches, banks, stores, a courthouse, newspapers, schools, railroads, and even an opera house. There were also more than a dozen saloons, a sheriff, and a jail for those who disturbed the peace of town life. The Diamond Match Company, with its two large sawmills, was the town's main employer. The company used some of the local pine to make its famous wooden matches but most was sawed into boards and shipped to the Midwest to be used for construction purposes. The company's two mills could together cut more than three hundred thousand feet of pine lumber a day.

Del Woodbury, left, was 16 years old in 1896 when a brush fire burned out of control and destroyed the city of Ontonagon. This photo was taken while he was being interviewed by Mort Neff of the Michigan Outdoors *television program in 1962.*

145

courtesy of Superior View, Marquette

For months during 1896, there had been small fires along the west side of the river, and the town's residents located on the river's east side had become accustomed to the smoky atmosphere. Now and again the smouldering fires crept close to the fences of the Diamond Match Company and to the log-sorting boom. Several times men had been sent out to work the fire lines, but no one was seriously concerned about the hazard. Everyone was simply too busy to worry about small fires over in the swamp.

On the morning of August 25th, a brisk southwest wind was rising. At 9:30 a.m. the Diamond Match foreman sent men out to check on the fires that were again reported to be close to the company's fences. Word came back that the situation was not serious. By noon, things had changed and the wind had reached gale force. Although the men who had families living on the west side of the river were concerned, they went to work at one o'clock, anyway.

In most industry when there's a fire in town and there are volunteer firemen working, they let the men go to the fire and come back when it's out. But that didn't happen that day. At one-fifteen, the fire whistle blew and both mills shut down, never to run again. The fire was coming out of the swamp in waves. Well, we all went across the river. We saw, but we couldn't do anything. There were ten or twelve houses on the west side and they were the first to catch fire. I headed straight for home because my father wasn't there. We lived up on the hill and it didn't look too bad there. I had three sisters, and I told my mother to bring their dresses and shoes and things which I would bury.

The fire had jumped to the town side of the river and into immense piles of lumber drying in the sun. Del estimated that more than 40 million feet of pine were burned that day. Soon the planing mill, the barn, the dry kiln, and the island mill were on fire. Flaming boards were hurled into the air by the tremendous heat rising from the lumber pile. The wind blew them over into the town, and the fire spread from wherever a board landed. People on the lower end of town (near the mouth of the river) were forced to the upper end where the roads left for Rockland and Greenland, two mining towns about a dozen miles away.

About three or four o'clock the wind changed and burning lumber was being blown all around. The fire finally drove us away, my mother, my sisters, and me. We went to the upper end of town

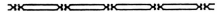

This old lithograph depicts On-tonagon before the 1896 fire.

photo courtesy of Ontonagon Historical Museum, Ontonagon

to the Greenland Road. I can't even venture to explain the scene that we saw when we got down to the ball field where the Greenland Road starts. The road was full of people and the vehicles they were taking. The smoke was so heavy you could see only a few feet. There was a fellow with a baby buggy full of stuff, a lady with a wagon filled with her belongings, a fellow leading a cow, and that's the way the whole town went. We walked a few more blocks and then we were out of the wind, which was so unpredictable that one house was on fire and the one next to it wasn't, just because of the path of the wind. An occasional house or row of houses was left standing when all the surrounding buildings were burned. We kept on going, but we didn't know where we were going; we were just getting away from the fire. Some fellow came along and said that the train was going to Rockland. Well, my mother's folks were living in Rockland. We got on the train and it didn't take long to load it. When we got there, it seemed that every house in Rockland took in people for the night. I was pretty happy when I got my mother and three sisters there to be with my grandparents. My grandfather worked down in the National Mine in Rockland and had to be at work at six in the morning. I got up when he did and I started back to Ontonagon on foot. I hitched a ride part way on the brewery wagon heading back into town to see if the brewery was still there. They had just bought the place and never got to sell a nickel's worth of beer. The brewery was gone.

Where the day before there was a pretty good little town going, what do you think I saw now? A little wisp of smoke once in awhile and the rest was ashes. I don't think there was a chimney standing in the whole downtown area. There were people scattered all around, some at the county poor farm and others at all the private farms outside of town. Of about 450 buildings, about 100 houses were left. The village president called a meeting and asked anyone who had friends or relatives out of town to go there.

When it was all over, the actual count of destroyed buildings was 344, but miraculously only one human life was lost. One elderly woman was unable to flee the blaze and two days later, a block from her home, she was found under some rubble.

There was a boat, The City of Straits, *on the south side of the bridge. She's at the bottom of the river yet. They'd have given anything to swing that bridge, but they didn't dare do that. People*

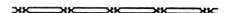

The photo above is a view of Ontonagon from the roof of the Diamond Match Company Store showing the north side of River Street before the 1896 fire.

photo courtesy of Ontonagon County Historical Museum

photo courtesy of Ontonagon County Historical Museum

⊃⊂⊃⊂⊃⊂⊃⊂⊃⊂⊃⊂

*The Ontonagon firemen, top pho-
to, could probably handle small
house or brush fires, but they were
no match for the raging fire that
swept out of the swamp and into
the town on August 25, 1896. The
eerie photograph at center shows
the still-smoldering remains of the
Diamond Match Company Store,
the West Side Mill, and the box
factory. Forty-eight hours after
the fire, the Ontonagon Bank of
C. Meilleur, bottom photo, was
open for business.*

photo courtesy of Ontonagon Historical Museum, Ontonagon

148

were using the bridge to escape the fire in that direction too. The boat burned to the waterline and sank in the river. They tell me the fishermen still hit it once in awhile. Another boat on the north side of the bridge was able to move out along the pier, out of range of the fire. I was told that when the fire swept by, the boat came back in and docked and fed a lot of people, and many slept on the decks for the night.

In 1896 there were few governmental agencies to come to the aid of people when disasters struck, so perhaps the most amazing story to come out of the fire was the generosity of the many individuals and companies who gave freely to help the victims.

The day after the fire, around ten o'clock, in comes a scow from the Nester Lumber Company in Baraga, loaded with supplies. It looked as though the town of Baraga had been cleaned out. There was even hay and oats for the town's livestock. Also that morning, the St. Paul came in [the railroad], and the telegraph tied into the lines that weren't burned on the edge of town. Once again we were hooked up with the outside world. The St. Paul declared a five-day suspension on all rates so that everything coming to Ontonagon was free. The same policy held for people who wanted to go away—no charge to anyone who wanted to go anywhere. The St. Paul brought in two sleeper cars, one loaded with blankets, which were distributed all over town. The next day, supplies commenced to arrive in railroad carloads. The first two cars contained Pillsbury flour and Gold Medal flour. The Diamond Match Company had been such a big buyer of supplies for its 55 lumber camps that many of its suppliers donated to the cause.

Donations came from all over and were dispersed to the townspeople from what was called the 'Gimme House.' Before any lumber arrived, the first Gimme House was set up in a barn on the edge of town. As lumber began to arrive another Gimme House was built in town. Everything that people wanted was donated—food, clothing, furniture, shoes, hay, and oats. On about the third day, the militia came in and put up 160 tents, a big mess tent, and a cook tent. My folks were still in Rockland, but I picked up two tents and put them together and cut the end out of one, for my family to live in. The railroad started bringing in lumber, so all the tents had board floors, but no heat. The light-colored canvas tents were called 'White City,' and they remained until late in the fall when most people started building new homes. Three days after the fire, I went back to where our house used to be and dug up the clothes I had buried. There was an old alarm clock I had buried with them and it was still running!

Before the *Herald* building had ceased smoking, F.J. Dirr, owner of the Ontonagon *Herald,* had telegraphed for a new press. The first issue after the fire, dated August 29, urged: "There are too many resources here to be abandoned and so we say to our citizens, cheer up, pull off your coats and go to work." Gradually, most of the town was rebuilt, but the Ontonagon operations of the Diamond Match Company remained closed. The peninsula's pine forests were beginning to give out and company bosses thought that the investment was not worth the trouble. Del Woodbury is no longer living and neither is anyone else who lived through the great Ontonagon fire, but thanks to their spirit, the town has survived.

photo courtesy of the Marquette County Historical Society, Marquette

One-Room Schools

One-room schoolhouses were scattered throughout the Upper Peninsula from the time families first ventured north in their search for iron and copper. They stood at crossroads, down wooded trails, or next to the general store, more or less evenly distributed with the population so that no student was required to walk more than three miles to school. They smelled unforgettably of chalk dust, apples, kids sweaty from playing recess hopscotch, and wool socks drying too close to the wood-burning stove. The schools were usually log cabins or tar paper shacks with cracks in the floor, separate boys' and girls' cloakrooms, benches that fit two pupils, gray chalkboards, and sometimes an awesome 10-foot-long recitation bench at the front of the room. On dreary days, children squinted in the lampless room, trying to make out the words of McGuffy's *Eclectic Reader* or deciphering five take away three. Some communities did not wait for a schoolhouse to be built before gathering the children together to drill them on the alphabet. During the summer of 1887, residents of Wakefield were concerned that their unattended children might be taken off by bears or other wild animals from the nearby woods. They located a teacher for the summer months, and, stretching a tent to protect students and teacher from the rain and sun, declared school in session. Norway's first school was held in a carpenter shop. School in Aura was conducted in an abandoned tar paper office building of the Hibbard Lumber Company. Many schools were conducted in private homes, and lighthouse keepers' children often had school in a room in the lighthouse living quarters. The Stalwart school board borrowed $50 to begin building a schoolhouse in 1882. They called for volunteers to help cut and hew logs for the 20 x 24-foot building, and paid Philip Waybrant to finish the job. Miss Evaline Hall was hired in at $20 a month for three months' teaching with a contract that called for "keeping a correct list of the pupils and their age and the number of days each pupil is present."

Covington Township held its first school from August 3 to November 16, 1894. Children ranged from ages 5 to 10 years, and Miss Hannah Shea from L'Anse drilled them on the three R's. The school paid Miss Shea $40 a month for three months, and paid $25 to the Robillards for the rent of one room of their home for the school. Edward Paquette was paid $7 for building the desks and seats, a bonus of $2 for building the blackboard, and $10.75 for room and board of the teacher. Paquette also purchased the school

Through the years, hundreds of children learned the three R's in this building. It is the Yalmer School in Marquette County.

photo courtesy of Janice Gerred, Lansing

BARAGA PUBLIC SCHOOLS

Report of *Liminga, Fannie*
Grade *Eight* For the Year 19*29* - 19*30*

	Sept.	Oct.	Nov.	Dec.	Jan.	Ex'm.	Av'k.	Feb.	Mar.	April	May	June	Ex'm.	Av'k.
Reading														
Spelling														
Writing	A	A	A		A	H	H	H	A	A	A			A
Language														
Physiology														
Geography														
Arithmetic	B	C	B	B	B	B	B	B+	B	B				
Grammar	A	A	A	A	A	A								
History	B	B	B+	A	A	A	B+	B+	b+	b+				
Government	B	B	B+	B+	B+	A	B	B	B	b+				
Agriculture	B	B+	B+	B+	A	B	B+							
Average														
Absent ½ days		1	0	1	0		5	2	2	1	0			
Times Tardy														
Citizenship	A	A	A	A	B		A	A	A	A	A			A

Ida Fitzpatrick Teacher.

(over)

broom, water pail, stove, and the wood, all for $25.

Art Lasanen's father grew tired of waiting for the township school board to provide a building for the six younger Lasanen children living at Small Traverse on the Keweenaw Peninsula. As the elder Mr. Lasanen made trips to Chassell to sell his fish, he would haul back all the lumber he could pile onto his fishing boat. During the summer of 1915, he brought back enough to build a schoolhouse. The township board hired Tillie Hendrickson Huldah to teach at a salary of $30 a month, and $5 to cover room and board with the Lasanens in their three-room log cabin. Miss Huldah slept with 14-year-old Mamie in a room with the other girls of the family, while the Lasanen boys bunked together in the summer kitchen.

In those early days, anyone who wished to become a teacher could be certified to conduct classes after six weeks of training from a recognized college. The teachers were often very young as some of them were accepted for the training program before they had completed high school. Mae Larson began attending school in 1915 when she was 12 years old, and quit when she was 20. "I was older than the teacher," she remembers, "and ashamed to go anymore." The instructors taught reading, writing, and arithmetic, along with any other skills they happened to possess, and many picked up additional training during the summer months, working toward the coveted Life Certificate. Teachers were often given a list of do's and don't's that strictly regulated their style of dress, and the extent to which they could socialize. Many were not allowed to drink, smoke, date, or dress in bright colors, and violating any of the rules could result in immediate dismissal. Most of the teachers took room and board with a family in the area.

"I didn't date while I was teaching at Petrell or Star Siding," recalls Ruth Henry of Munising, "but I don't think the school board would have liked it if I had. They kept track of what I did."

"A teacher had to watch her dress and stick with browns, blacks and grays," adds Amanda Wiljanen Larson who taught in a one-room school in 1929. "We were never allowed to wear red; it denoted communism. Shoes were oxfords—sensible and practical— and our behavior had to be above reproach."

Above, Fannie Liminga was a good student and only missed 10 half days all year. She completed the eighth grade at Baraga Public School with a B-plus average, and teacher Ida Fitzpatrick wrote "Promoted" across Fannie's report card. Above right, children of all ages learned together in a one-room school.

photo courtesy of Superior View, Marquette

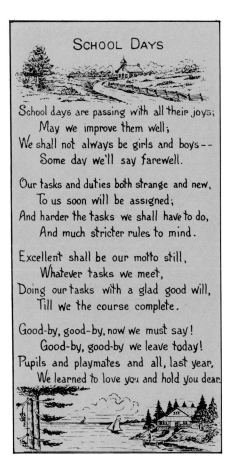

SCHOOL DAYS

School days are passing with all their joys;
  May we improve them well;
We shall not always be girls and boys--
  Some day we'll say farewell.

Our tasks and duties both strange and new,
  To us soon will be assigned;
And harder the tasks we shall have to do,
  And much stricter rules to mind.

Excellent shall be our motto still,
  Whatever tasks we meet,
Doing our tasks with a glad good will,
  Till we the course complete.

Good-by, good-by, now we must say!
  Good-by, good-by we leave today!
Pupils and playmates and all, last year,
  We learned to love you and hold you dear.

School days usually lasted eight hours and often the younger students fell asleep at their desks before the day was through. As in schools everywhere, the girls and boys teased each other when they thought the teacher wasn't looking. A dunce cap was kept handy for those who were caught, or punishment beyond horrors, a *boy* was made to sit in the same seat with a *girl*. Many children, especially in the western and central Upper Peninsula, attended school before they could speak English. To assist those whose native tongue was German, Finnish, Swedish, or Italian, several objects throughout the room were labeled in English, such as CHAIR, DESK, and BLACKBOARD. Dora Mili, who taught school west of Baraga beginning in 1919, remembers that young children unable to speak English came to school and "just sat there. It was difficult to even get their names for the first few days," she recalls.

Students marched into their schools each morning at the sounding of a bell. Some schools were fortunate to have large bells which hung from a belfrey located either on top of the schoolhouse or in the school yard. The Pioneer School in Skandia had the belfrey, but never was able to secure a bell. Kids found uses for the empty belfrey, however. According to Clarence Specker, who attended classes in the school around 1920, the belfrey offered a spectacular view of Skandia and the surrounding farmland.

"You could see the whole area," he says, remembering his boyhood. "The air felt good out there, and it was a great place to hide from a teacher. Unfortunately, we lost some of our playtime as punishment for climbing up without permission."

In one corner of every schoolroom stood a big wood-burning stove. Children seated nearest the stove all but sizzled from the heat, while those farthest away shivered in the cold. Far corners of the room were often unbearably chilly, with frost on the windows and drafty winds howling underneath the door and through the cracks of the unvarnished floor. Small fingers were sometimes too cold to hold a pencil. Students without woolen socks or swampers (some children were forbidden to wear swampers in school because almost every mother agreed it resulted in bad eyesight!) shuffled their feet restlessly to ward off pain in their numbing toes, and

These bright children with their high-button shoes and stern expressions were photographed by J. W. Nara in Calumet about 1910. The students were told to hold very still for the long exposure time, but sometimes they moved just a little (perhaps they were tickled) and the resulting picture would show ghost-like blurs.

153

photo courtesy of Marquette County Historical Society

longed for their caps hanging from pegs in the cloakroom.

The task of fire-building and water-hauling in the early morning hours fell to either a hired janitor, the teacher, or one of the older students. Water was fetched from an outdoor pump and left in a community bucket on a table in the back of the room. Students each took their turn at the water dipper, sometimes having to break through a layer of ice before they could take a drink. Before the children learned to make their own paper cups, the community dipper was often responsible for the spreading of childhood illnesses. Remembers one former student, "If one of us got the mumps, we all got the mumps." Students brought lunch in lard pails or paper bags crammed full of substantial sandwiches, apples in season, and milk in old vanilla bottles or mason jars. During the winter months, pails were placed next to the stove to prevent lunches freezing in the cloakroom. On sunny spring days, lunch was eaten at the school cafeteria—on top of the woodpile.

Attendance at one-room schools was often not very regular. In some schools, students could begin attending class any month of the year, and one school allowed children to start as soon as they reached the age of five, whether their birthday came in September or May. The harsh winters kept some children home, as did planting season, silo-filling, potato-picking, and a variety of other activities throughout the year. Those who made it to school during the winter months sometimes hopped rides in the family cutter or sleigh, bundled in robes up to their noses. Some of the students in Pickford arrived by dog sled. The Granskog family in Stonington operated the first school bus in Delta County in 1920, and one account said it "looked like a fish shanty on a sled, with a driver's seat in the middle." Many children skied or snowshoed, and took shortcuts across frozen lakes. Irja Harju and her brother from L'Anse ran a trapline for weasels and muskrats as they made their way through the woods. In the mid-1930s, when public school transportation was introduced, Ernest Johnson operated his Oldsmobile station wagon as a Skandia school bus, with more than 20 kids to a load. "They

This is the Otter Lake School Bus whose lucky riders could forgo the long walks to and from school.

photo courtesy of Marquette County Historical Society

were so crammed in," he recalls, "they couldn't turn their heads."

Teaching several different subjects to a room full of children of varying ages and attendance records required a lot of juggling. Amanda Larson remembers how she handled it. You may think the concept of teacher's aids are new but, "I had them then," she recalls. "While I taught reading, an older girl took another class into the cloak room to tutor them on arithmetic."

School wasn't all hard work and drills. Some schools had a piano or organ and Earl Willette, who began his 44-year teaching career in Laird Township in 1933, remembers, "Once a week, we took an hour off just to sing."

Recess and lunch hours were special times, with games of jump rope, baseball, hide-and-seek, marbles, tag, hopscotch, Red-Rover, cat and dog, and king of the hill. Planning for the annual Christmas program also afforded some fun. In addition to practicing lines for the pageant, and making costumes from flour sacks and cardboard, the children and teacher would go to a nearby woods to cut a Christmas tree. From December until spring, older students frantically studied for the state's 8th Grade exam which had to be passed before continuing to high school. For many, 8th grade marked the end of formal education.

One-room-schoolhouse indelible impressions include: the tardy bell, spelling bees, arithmetic books with the answers in the back, the school woodshed, trying to squeeze bare feet into new school shoes, measles, mumps and chicken pox, ink wells and scratchy pens for "good work," orthography, the endless push and pull of Palmer Penmanship, recitation, declamation, oratorical contests, Valentines made with construction paper and flour-water paste, the end-of-school picnic, and the coldest place in the world—an outdoor school privy. At last, after the terrifying walks up the aisle to receive monthly report cards, after exams when answers failed to come, there was the joy of running home with arms flung wide, with end-of-the-year report card in hand, to stand in the door panting and shout for all the world to hear, "I passed!"

As the Upper Peninsula grew in population, larger schools were built and children were grouped according to age and ability. This photograph of a 1st grade classroom was taken in Baraga in 1915.

155

photo courtesy of Marquette County Historical Society, Marquette

Ivory Towers

On the eve of the Civil War in 1860, the census for the Upper Peninsula was a mere 18,000 residents. Although institutions of higher learning were developing in the Lower Peninsula, educational programs beyond the most rudimentary sort seemed hardly worth consideration in the U.P. But conditions were changing. The potential for growth in the U.P.'s mining regions was obvious, and it was evident that better-trained personnel would be needed to take full advantage of these resources. Too many mining ventures were failing for lack of mining expertise.

Legislative Act 207, "to establish and regulate a mining school in the Upper Peninsula, at or near the village of Houghton," was signed by Governor Austin Blair on March 15, 1861. Had this act been implemented, the current Michigan Technological University would have had the distinction of being the first mining school in the United States. Instead, the Civil War intervened shortly after the passage of the act, and the project was delayed for 25 years.

The idea, however, was not forgotten. In 1864, a school of mines was established in Ann Arbor, and by 1867 the first degrees had been conferred in the program by the University of Michigan. The program was temporarily halted because the demand for engineers was not great, and because Ann Arbor was so far from the copper and iron mining of the U.P. But by the 1880s, there was a serious shortage of men who were trained in ore extraction and processing, and leaders of the mining industry became concerned.

State Senator Jay A. Hubbell took the first steps toward establishing a separate mining school in Michigan by steering a bill through the legislature which provided an appropriation of $25,000 for "equipment and maintenance" of the Michigan Mining School. The board unanimously chose to locate the school at Houghton, close to the burgeoning mining activities, so students could combine theoretical with practical knowledge. Senator Hubbell secured an additional appropriation of $75,000 for a suitable building, and donated real estate for that purpose from his own property on the eastern edge of the village.

Classes were convened in the fall of 1886 in rented quarters above the Houghton fire engine house. Twenty-three pupils were enrolled, although only seven were in the projected two-year curriculum leading to a bachelor of science in mining. That first year was nearly a disaster, and Principal Albert Williams, Jr. resigned after completion of the course work. Dr. Marshman Wadsworth

At left is the Houghton Town Hall, first home of Michigan Technological University.

photo courtesy of Michigan Technological University
Archives and Copper Country Historical Collections

MICHIGAN COLLEGE
OF MINES

photo courtesy of Superior View, Marquette

was persuaded to leave the staff of Colby College in Maine and become director of the Michigan Mining School. With little time to reorganize for a second year of operation, Wadsworth worked miracles collecting a staff and students, while at the same time strengthening the curriculum. In spite of community pessimism, enrollment gradually increased, the course of study was lengthened to three years, and a new building was completed in 1889. Wadsworth was aggressive in seeking funding from the legislators, and by the summer of 1890, the school was, he said, "firmly established as a constituent part of the higher education of the state of Michigan never to be uprooted or destroyed."

His words proved true even when, shortly thereafter, the Democrats came to power and targeted the school for closure in an attempt to reverse what they regarded as the profligate tendencies of state government. The Michigan Mining School soon became the largest mining school in the nation. In 1896, the University of Michigan terminated its program in mining engineering, and the following year Michigan Mining School became the Michigan College of Mines. When the need for mining engineers decreased, the school broadened its goals. In 1927, it became the Michigan College of Mining and Technology, and was renamed Michigan Technological University in 1964. In 1916, at the second reunion of graduates from the Michigan College of Mines, Dr. Wadsworth reminisced about the difficulty of keeping alive the small school he had been called upon to save in 1887. He declared, "The rain descended, and floods came, and the winds blew and beat upon the house, and it fell not, for it was founded upon a rock, in the hearts of the northern peninsula."

Recognizing the need for a teachers' college in the Upper Peninsula, State Senator Peter White of Marquette worked on legislation in 1875 to authorize the development of a "normal school" in Marquette. Because of strong opposition by both the University of Michigan and Michigan State Normal School, it failed to get through the legislature. Michigan Normal, located in Ypsilanti, was the first such institution west of the Alleghenies and, as it was struggling for survival, it had little desire to see competitors organized

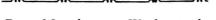

Dr. Marshman Wadsworth, above, was president of the Michigan Mining School from 1887-1899. He increased enrollment, lengthened the course of study, and sought legislative funding for the school. In 1897, it was renamed the Michigan College of Mines, above right.

158

photo by Childs Art Gallery, courtesy of Superior View, Marquette

photo by J.W. Nara, courtesy of Superior View, Marquette

elsewhere. By the 1890s, the need for a normal school in the northern part of the state had become so acute that the issue was revived. Several communities in both the Upper and Lower Peninsulas actively sought support for the right to become the location selected, but the citizens of Mount Pleasant initiated action and started their own private normal school—Central Normal. The program and facilities were taken over by the state in 1895, once again delaying the development of such a school in the U.P.

Central Normal did not increase the number of trained teachers in the far north, where they were needed. For the 50,000 school children in the Upper Peninsula, there were about 1,200 teachers, of whom only 300 had had any formal training beyond high school.

Legislation for Marquette Normal finally passed on April 28, 1899. In an early example of "local match," the people of Marquette were expected to raise $5,000 for the equipment in the new school. The voters decisively approved the necessary bond issue, and by September 19, 1899, thirty-two students were enrolled for classes in rented quarters in the city.

Although early stages of the normal school were not as filled with uncertainty as those of the mining school, there were some crucial questions about administration that briefly jeopardized the independence of the institution. Marquette Normal, also called Northern, was initially under the direct control of the State Board of Education, with a single president for all campuses of the normal schools. Annoyed by such actions, the *Daily Mining Journal* in Marquette penned an editorial which asked, "Have We Been Buncoed?" saying that the board was composed only of Lower Peninsula men who were probably trying to make Northern a feeder school for Ypsilanti. Although the board gave reassurance that Northern would be equal in rank to Ypsilanti, Marquette Northern was not authorized to grant life certificates until 1902.

Dwight B. Waldo, formerly on the staff of Albion College, was chosen first principal of the new school. He was so effective that in 1904, he was sent to head the next established normal school which was located in Kalamazoo. Northern's summer sessions had greater enrollment than the regular school year—a reflection of the fact

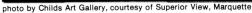

In 1896, the Finnish Evangelical Lutheran Church—Suomi Synod founded the Finnish college Suomi-Opisto, above, in Hancock. Above left is an early picture of Longyear Hall at Northern Normal School in Marquette. The school grew rapidly and its name changes reflected the curriculum diversification. In 1963, it became Northern Michigan University.

photo courtesy of Michigan Technological University Archives and Copper Country Historical Collections

photo courtesy of Michigan Technological University Archives and Copper Country Historical Collections

Those are Michigan Mining School students in the top photograph. When Michigan Tech had no coeds, male students had to play the female characters in dramatic roles. Those in the center photo are cast members from the play "A Lucky Break." Herb Hawn, fourth from left, became the school's first "campus queen" and later served on the faculty for years. The bottom photograph is of the first graduating class of Suomi College.

photo courtesy of Suomi College

160

that many students were already teaching—and the student body was almost exclusively female. With legislative support, Northern gradually upgraded its program and increased the requirements for graduation. By 1920 the institution was authorized to grant a bachelor's degree, and in 1927, its name was changed to Northern State Teachers College. The school had by then become the focal point of pedagogy in the Upper Peninsula. Further diversification of the curriculum was reflected in another change of name in 1941—Northern Michigan College of Education. After the Second World War, particularly during the late 1950s, Northern grew rapidly to become the largest state school in the U.P. In 1963 it became Northern Michigan University, but to some old-timers it will always be "Marquette Normal" or "the Teachers' College."

During the latter part of the Nineteenth Century, so many Finnish immigrants came to the U.P. that they made up the peninsula's largest single ethnic group. As they congregated into tightly-knit communities, the Finns revealed an associative spirit that led them to organize churches, temperance societies, cultural and nationalistic clubs, cooperatives and, a bit later, labor associations. Liberated from the restrictions of a state church in Finland, those Finns who were church-minded divided into several smaller sects such as the Finnish Evangelical Lutheran Church—Suomi Synod, founded in 1890 by several congregations, primarily in the Copper Country. In 1896, they founded the Finnish college Suomi-Opisto.

Although Suomi did not have to face the obstacles confronted by the public schools, the idea of such a school was not universally welcomed by the Finnish immigrants who saw the church as being greedy or extravagant. The leaders of the church, however, wanted to establish a college because of the need to train additional clergymen. They also had nationalist and cultural reasons as Finland was then a part of Tsarist Russia, and most Finnish people, regardless of political and ideological differences, dreamed of an independent Finland. The school opened in the fall of 1896 in west Hancock with only eleven students. Under the guidance of the Rev. Juho K. Nikander, president of both the Synod and the college until his death in 1919, Suomi began to grow.

There was general agreement that Suomi-Opisto was for Finnish immigrants and their descendants, and that its purpose was to preserve their religion, heritage, and culture. The first students passed through a series of "grades," modeled upon a Finnish lyceum plan, and were graduated in 1904. Eventually, however, the school was modified to become the equivalent of an American secondary school. In 1923, a junior college department was organized which, along with the popular commercial courses, began to attract non-Finns to the institution. The metamorphosis of Suomi into a more typical church-related American college was not accomplished easily. The change was strongly contested by those who wished it to remain a "Finn school," and there was discussion about Suomi's role in higher education for the Lutheran church in the United States. In 1958, the theological seminary, which was for many the main reason for continuing the institution, was transferred to a larger school in Chicago. A few years later, Suomi Synod merged into the newly formed Lutheran Church in America.

But Suomi College survived these drastic changes and since

photo courtesy of Suomi College

photo courtesy of Marquette County Historical Society

then has grown in enrollment and gained regional accreditation. While the character of the school is no longer that of a small immigrant college, its name symbolizes the contribution of an immigrant people to the education and culture of the nation.

Other attempts to establish private schools of higher education were not as successful. Jordan College of Menominee, and Mackinac College on Mackinac Island represented the most serious efforts, and for a while they both seemed to have a fighting chance. Jordan was a Roman Catholic school under the auspices of the Fathers of the Society of the Divine Savior. Opened in 1932, the school was plagued with financial problems, and enrollment was only slightly more than 100 students each year, declining to less that 70 in 1938-39. During the seven years it was open, Jordan College graduated 39 students from its four-year program. The school's impact, however, cannot be measured in numbers of graduates alone. Although it was a small coeducational institution with a high percentage of women, the school's athletic teams, the Jordan College Angels, achieved a reputation as a sort of small-college Notre Dame. During one successful season the team reached competition in a national tournament.

After World War II, Mackinac Island became a major location for Moral Re-Armament. By 1956, MRA had built a sizeable facility for conferences at Cedar Point in the southeastern section of the island, where members gathered primarily in the summer months. The potential for making year-round use of the excellent complex was a motivating factor in planning for a college, and when MRA directors agreed to turn over the properties to the proposed education corporation known as Mackinac College, permission was granted from the State Board of Education. First instruction began in 1966. Because of backing from influential people in the MRA movement, the outlook seemed promising for a private college in such an historic setting. But the college could not attract enough students or gain enough financial support and it folded. In 1970, some loyal students became the only graduates of the institution.

The Upper Peninsula's first junior college was started in Calumet in 1929. But the Depression was felt strongly in the Copper Country, and in 1932 the program ended. One community that suc-

In 1913, the Suomi College basketball team, above, posed for this studio photograph. The proper ladies above right were studying at the library of Northern Normal when this photo was taken in the early 1900s.

cessfully defied the Depression was Ironwood, the major population center on the Gogebic Range. Classes began in 1932 at facilities in the local high school and, although the declining economy almost forced the school to close in 1938, concerned individuals and somewhat reluctant support from the county kept the doors open. During that time its name was changed to Gogebic Junior College. After barely surviving the war years, the institution began to prosper, as did many of the other schools when returning veterans increased enrollments. As the community's educational needs changed, Gogebic shifted into vocational programs. By 1966, it was reorganized into Gogebic Community College and a few years later it moved to a new campus north of the city.

In April 1963, the Bay de Noc Community College was established to serve the needs of the Escanaba-Gladstone area. This institution typified the modern version of a two-year college, with a commitment to meeting a variety of community needs. It is evident that the time and place were ideal for Bay de Noc because it did not have to weather opposition of the magnitude that had earlier beset other schools in other areas.

Throughout the years, several specialized institutions have been launched in various communities of the Upper Peninsula. Not necessarily on the collegiate level, they provided training for many skills. One of the most interesting was Menominee County Agricultural College, founded in 1907 to serve a region considered to contain the most valuable agricultural lands in the peninsula. The college operated a farm to provide practical experience for its students. Graduates became agricultural agents or farmers, and in some years, enrollment was as high as 60 students. The school depended on state aid for a large part of its support, however, and when that was terminated in 1929, the college was forced to close. The facility was taken over and utilized by the Michigan Military Academy, a private military school for boys. Perhaps the only such institution to have existed in the Upper Peninsula, it failed to get adequate support and lasted only one school year, 1930-31.

Business colleges opened to provide trained personnel for the local business community. Such names as Twin City Business College, Cloverland College, and Laurium Commercial College may bring back memories for some scholars. But when other institutions entered the field, primarily high schools offering commercial courses, the once common business colleges began to disappear.

While the western and central parts of the U.P. were reasonably well served by institutions of higher education, the same opportunities were not available in eastern communities such as Sault Ste. Marie, Newberry, and St. Ignace until after World War II. In 1946, the Sault Ste. Marie residence center of the Michigan College of Mining and Technology opened. The Sault branch was designed as a feeder to the Houghton campus, and also provided junior college services to students not interested in engineering. The school grew to a four-year program, and by 1967, the first bachelor's degree candidates were graduated from what had been renamed Lake Superior State College of Michigan Technological University. On January 1, 1970, Lake Superior State became an independent institution. Today, higher education taught by qualified instructors is available in nearly every corner of the Upper Peninsula.

photo courtesy of Marquette County Historical Society

Taming The St. Mary's

The first Chippewa migrated to the rapids of the St. Mary's River in the Sixteenth Century. After discovering bountiful quantities of fine whitefish inhabiting the turbulent water, they established a permanent village at the rapids' edge. The Indians named the whitefish *Addik-kim-maig,* or deer of the waters, in tribute to its importance as a food source. When missionary Father Claude Dablon visited the area in 1689, he described the fish as "very white and very excellent." The river and the whitefish largely sustained the Chippewa and their way of life until 19th and 20th Century lock projects put an end to the rapids' use as a primary fishing ground. The surrounding area was settled and developed, and today it is the principal city of the eastern Upper Peninsula.

Early French explorers named the location Sault de Sainte Marie, "sault" being the French word for falling water. Prior to the opening of the locks, ship cargo had to be unloaded by hand, portaged around the rapids, then reloaded by hand onto another boat. Sometimes the boat itself was portaged around the rapids. Although the portage work was backbreaking and slow, it required considerable labor and provided many jobs in the Sault. When Michigan achieved statehood in 1837, its first governor, Stevens T. Mason, urged the legislature to provide for a passage through the rapids. But at the time the state could not afford to take on the project. It was clear that only the federal government had the money to build such a canal. The portage was made somewhat easier in 1839 when a strap railroad was built by the American Fur Company. Horses and mules pulled carts from a warehouse near the foot of present day Bingham Street along Water Street west to River, where the line curved to Portage Street and extended to the head of the rapids. About 1846, McKnight Bros. & Tinker took over the operation of the railway, followed by the Chippewa Portage Company. In 1850, the company transferred 6,000 tons of cargo around the rapids at a charge of one dollar per ton.

With trade and population growing in the 1840s and '50s, commerce on Lakes Ontario, Erie, Huron, and Michigan was burgeoning, but Lake Superior remained relatively inaccessible. During the 1840s, the iron ore and copper mined in the Upper Peninsula's midsection was held up for months while the portage workers moved it around the rapids. The portage business, however, was an important local industry, and community opinion opposed the construction of the locks, which would put an end to portage jobs. After a

The locks made Lake Superior accessible to passenger and cargo ships. This early photo shows the Saronic *passing through.*

photo courtesy of Materna Studio, Sault Ste. Marie

photo by Childs Art Gallery, courtesy of Materna Studio, Sault Ste. Marie

The top photo shows Old Fort Brady at the Soo. At center is Water Street which became part of the route of the strap railroad built in 1839 to ease portaging. The bottom photo is a very early view of the locks with sailing vessels passing through.

photo courtesy of Marquette County Historical Society

decade and a half of lobbying against sometimes strong Congressional opposition, those in favor of the canal got what they wanted. In 1852, President Millard Fillmore signed a bill authorizing a lock at the St. Mary's rapids to be 250 feet in length, 60 feet in width, and 12 feet in depth. Later the dimensions were altered so that when completed the length was 350 feet. In spite of all the preconstruction adversity, the State Lock was completed in June, 1855, and one of the world's richest agricultural and industrial regions soon developed around the Great Lakes.

The company which built the lock was formed by a group of eastern financiers. Known as the St. Mary's Falls Ship Canal Company, it was to be paid not in cash but in 750,000 acres of Michigan land. The lock was completed on time, and it has been widely assumed that its first superintendent, Charles T. Harvey, deserves the credit. However, recent research has shown that the company officers were dissatisfied with Harvey within six months, and by the end of 1853, he had fallen behind schedule. In May, 1854, he was demoted, and John W. Davis was given the responsibility of completing the project. But history takes strange turns. Harvey had the good fortune to outlive the others involved in building the lock, and when Sault Ste. Marie celebrated the fiftieth anniversary of the State Lock in 1905, Harvey attended the celebration and was praised for his accomplishment.

Soon after completion of the first lock, it became evident that a second lock was needed, so the 515-foot Weitzel Lock was built on the Michigan side of the State Lock and opened in 1881. Ironically, while Harvey was being honored at the 50th anniversary celebration, the State Lock no longer existed. It had been destroyed in 1888 to make way for the expansive Poe Lock. Named after Civil War colonel Orlando M. Poe, the 704-foot-long lock had been completed in 1896. Both the Weitzel and Poe, however, proved inadequate for the shipping needs of the Twentieth Century. They were joined by two new locks, called the Davis and the Sabin. These locks are of equal size, 1350 feet long and 80 feet wide, and still in use today. They share the same canal approach and extend farthest from the American shore. In 1941, work began on the 800-foot-long MacArthur Lock which was to replace the Weitzel Lock. It was completed in just fifteen months.

With the advent of bigger ships in the Great Lakes, all the existing locks were too small. Although the Davis and Sabin were long enough at 1350 feet, they were only 80 feet wide. The Poe Lock was wide enough at 100 feet, but was only 704 feet in length, and at 800 feet, the MacArthur Lock was obviously not long enough. The oldest of the existing locks, the Poe, was sacrificed, and after nearly seven years in construction, the second Poe Lock was completed in 1968. It measures 1200 feet in length and 110 feet in width, and can easily accommodate the latest generation of "lakers."

No one can dispute the locks' success. Only two months after the State Lock opened, the first iron ore from the Upper Peninsula passed through on the *Columbia*. In 1856, the first full year of shipping, 11,597 tons of Upper Peninsula iron ore passed through the lock. By 1862, the total had reached 113,014. Later, when Minnesota's vast Mesabi Range was opened, iron ore shipments increased. During that time, more than 100 million tons of iron ore each year poured out of the Mesabi Range for passage through the Soo Locks, a total greater than the combined tonnage that went through the Panama and Suez canals. During World War II, the heavily guarded locks were considered critical to the Allied war effort.

A pumping station to bring water from the St. Mary's into Sault homes was built in 1886, and the beginnings of a telephone system were installed in the city in 1869. In May, 1887, the Ste. Mary's Falls Water Power Company obtained the right-of-way for the construction of a canal along the St. Mary's River to harness the potential in its 21-foot drop. When it was completed in 1902, the canal became the source of the city's electricity. To use the power, D.B. Henderson of Dubuque, Iowa obtained a city franchise for an electro-lighting company. Also in 1887, work was begun on the city's sewage system, and the Sault obtained state recognition as a chartered city. The following year, its first city council was elected and Democrat George Brown became the city's first mayor.

Real estate in 1887 was selling for fantastic prices, bringing instant wealth to some. In their history of the Saint Mary's River, *River of Destiny*, authors Joseph and Estelle Bayliss reported that a log house on Portage Street in that year sold for $31,500; just twenty years earlier, it sold for $386. In 1887, the value of all the Sault's buildings was $1,208,000, whereas the previous year, the value had been only $43,000. By the year's end, the real estate boom had subsided, but prosperity held. As the city developed, the business center grew up within a three-block section of Water Street, which ran parallel to the river. In August 1896, a fire gutted Water Street, causing about $325,000 in damage. The center of downtown was permanently rebuilt on Portage and Ashmun Streets.

The Sault had a number of enthusiastic boosters in the 1880s and '90s. Probably the most notable was Chase Osborn who moved to the city in 1887 at the age of 27. Arriving with a background in journalism, Osborn and two others purchased the weekly *Chippewa County News* from William Chandler and Company. In 1892, Osborn purchased the Sault's other paper, the *Sault de Sainte Marie Tribune* and consolidated it with the *News*. Within a short time, Osborn became extremely wealthy, not because of the newspaper business, but as a result of his discovery and purchase of iron deposits near Sudbury, Ontario.

In the 1890s, Osborn wrote a pamphlet entitled "The Soo, the New Metropolis," subtitled "The Coming City of the Great Lakes, the Gem of the New North." Predicting a great future for the Sault, Osborn wrote:

The "Soo" with its key-like location, its grandest water-power in the world, its great locks, the bracing, cooling, exhilarating, healing atmosphere, the solidity that characterizes its present rapid growth, the coming of transcontinental railways, the hundreds of large vessels that pass its great canals daily, the vast local and governmental improvements projected and under way, its unsurpassed agricultural resources, great forest resources, extensive mineral deposits close at hand, splendid school system and local government, elegant churches of many denominations, and many other things that constitute the foundation of a great metropolis, will be a city of 25,000 inhabitants within three years, and its great growth will not cease or diminish.

photo courtesy of Marquette County Historical Society

photo courtesy of Marquette County Historical Society

When Osborn wrote this forecast, the city was approaching the 1900 federal census, which recorded a population of 10,538. His three-year prediction was not reached in three years, or even in ten, for by 1910, the population had increased by only about 2,000.

Still, optimism was not unjustified in these years. The Sault was a rough frontier town at the turn of the century, and even its underworld was prosperous. One observer noted that brothels, gambling dens, and saloons where all thriving. For its population of 10,000, some historic accounts claim that the Sault had 87 saloons. A Michigan law later limited the number of a city's saloons to one for every 500 residents.

Osborn's optimism was based on more substantial enterprises than saloons, however. Larger businesses were coming to the city. Shortly after 1890, the Soo Woolen Mills was established to supply the Upper Peninsula timber industry with wool clothing. Nearby sheep farms in Chippewa County provided the mill with its raw material. In 1899, the Northwestern Leather Company opened on the St. Mary's shore above the locks, enjoying the advantages of

Top and bottom, as larger ships began passing through the Soo, larger locks had to be built to accommodate them.

169

clean river water and the bark of nearby hemlock trees, both essential to the tanning process. The Edison Sault Electric Company was formed in 1892. To take advantage of the power canal, Union Carbide opened operations in the Sault in 1903, becoming the first manufacturing company to utilize the city's hydro power. Later, Union Carbide built a plant on the east side of the powerhouse, fronting the St. Mary's River.

Crusading newspaper publisher Frank Knox arrived at the Sault in 1902. In April of that year, he began publishing the *Evening Journal,* a Republican paper dedicated to clean government. He was so successful that in slightly more than a year, he conquered the opposition *News-Record* and took over its plant. One of his supporters was Chase Osborn who was by then out of the newspaper business. Knox was chairman of Michigan's Republican Central Committee and he helped elect Osborn to the governorship in 1910.

Chase Osborn is the only person from the U.P. to have served Michigan as governor, and the Osborn home still stands on Cedar Street. Frank Knox ran as Republican vice-presidential candidate with Alf Landon in 1936 and served as President Roosevelt's Secretary of the Navy during World War II.

The Sault's rapid growth was completed by the early years of the 20th Century. During the 1920s, Sault Ste. Marie had twelve factories and was served by fifteen passenger steamship lines. The city's principal enterprises weathered the depression years of the 1930s and went on to further prosperity during World War II. But there was one unapparent flaw in the Sault's developing economy. Its industrial base was outside owned and outside controlled. In the late 1950s, the Sault's industrial base began to collapse.

The first major employer to close was the Soo Woolen Mills, in January, 1955. The equipment of this Saginaw-based company was sold and the plant was razed. In March, 1956, the board of the Cadillac-Soo Lumber Company announced it would close up its Sault operations the following June. Our Own Bakeries, with operations in both Marquette and the Sault, decided in December, 1956, to close its Sault plant and combine both operations in Marquette. Before the end of 1956, Lock City Marine and Machine ter-

photo courtesy of Janice Gerred, Lansing

This boat, one of the famed whalebacks, is shown leaving the Poe Lock.

170

minated its 200 employees and ceased operation.

The Sault's two largest employers—Northwestern Leather with about 850 employees, and Union Carbide with 600, also shut down. Northwestern Leathers was closed after a wage dispute was not successfully negotiated. Union Carbide began having economic difficulties in 1956 and reduced its employees by 100. One reason given for the difficulties was that natural gas was increasingly being used in place of acetylene in the development of chemicals. Since the Sault plant was acetylene-based, its profits were adversely affected. The New York-based company did not get requested tax relief from the city, and closed its Sault plant in November, 1963.

Since Union Carbide's departure, the Sault has not had another large industry. Although a few small industries exist, the city's economic base is now largely government and tourism. The U.S. Army Corps of Engineers, which maintains the locks, and the four-year Lake Superior State College with its nearly 2500 students, are among the largest payrolls in the city.

To tourists, the locks symbolize the Sault, but they also symbolize what has caused some of the city's greatest problems. Since 1881, when the federal government took over operation of the locks from the State of Michigan, no tolls have been collected from ships utilizing the locks. Since the locks are federally owned and controlled, they are operated for the benefit of the country as a whole, not necessarily for the benefit of the Sault. As Phil Bellfy stressed in his 1981 Master's thesis at M.S.U., "The lock system was in no way intended to serve the interests of the Sault, indeed, it had the opposite effect: from its inception it was intended to move goods *through* the Sault faster and cheaper." As with the locks, so with the manufacturing industries. The largest businesses in the Sault were without local ownership, and they eventually left. Before the locks, this was not the case. When years ago the Chippewa, and later the portage workers at the rapids, controlled their own resources, they prospered. If there is a lesson to be learned here, perhaps it is that to thrive and grow and to fulfill the prophecies of its early supporters, the Sault needed a sound, locally-owned economy based on its own bountiful resources.

photo courtesy of Chippewa County Historical Society

Flag-strewn ships and a crowd of well-wishers marked this day of celebration at the locks at Sault Ste. Marie.

171

photo courtesy of Superior View, Marquette

WINNERS!

With their muscles made strong by the rigors of life in the wild north country, early Upper Peninsula residents pursued athletics with built-in strength and determination. Across the peninsula, clubs were formed to link together enthusiasts of particular activities such as snowshoeing, walking, and bicycling. And while some participated in sports just for the fun of it, many others had a powerful desire to *win*. The greatest of those have achieved regional, state, national, and even world recognition, and their feats are being recorded in the Upper Peninsula Sports Hall of Fame. Located at Northern Michigan University in Marquette, the Hall of Fame was organized in 1971 and inducts ten new members each year in a dedicated effort to acknowledge the athletic achievements of Upper Peninsula men and women.

Boxing was illegal when Hillman-born Frank Adams was growing up, but that didn't stop him from becoming a fighter. He even changed his name to Kid Parker to keep the career a secret from his father, who expected young Frank to pursue a more respectable trade. Nominated to the Hall of Fame in 1981, Parker survived 111 fights without a knockdown, and was a 1904 contender for the world lightweight boxing championship. His last fight, against Detroit's Jimmy Fredy, took place in 1914 on a scow in the St. Mary's River in an unsuccessful attempt to elude the sheriff.

Beginning in the early 1870s, a favorite pastime in U.P. mining towns was Cornish wrestling. Two- and three-day tournaments were scheduled throughout the summer months, especially around the 4th of July, and some towns even built special wrestling parks. In 1887, Marquette sponsored a three-day tournament starring Evan "The Strangler" Lewis. Lewis was challenged by Harry James of Negaunee, and a $100 purse was promised to the winner of three falls out of five. More than 700 spectators pushed and shoved for a better view as 70-year-old referee Tom Carkeek climbed into the 40-foot sawdust ring. Carkeek knew Cornish wrestling well—he had 582 matches under his *own* belt. Lewis and James weighed in on the ringside scale at under the legal 180 pounds. They were dressed according to the Redruth Rules of Cornish Wrestling; barefoot, knee breeches or trunks, loose canvas jackets with strong collars and cuffs, and sleeves the regulation 18 to 22 inches in length. The men shook hands and came out grabbing "catch-as-can" the other's jacket. All holds were allowed except cross-collar or two collars in one hand. "No butting, scratching, or striking," ruled

At left, Tauno Nurmela proudly displays some of the ribbons and cups he won during his legendary career in track and field events.

photo courtesy of Ski Hall of Fame, Ishpeming

photo courtesy of Marquette County Historical Society

Carkeek. If a wrestler touched his hands to the ground to break his fall *once*, Carkeek called a foul. If he touched *twice*, Carkeek called a fall. A legal fall came when a wrestler was thrown to his back with two hips and one shoulder, or two shoulders and one hip touching the ground. The Strangler was victorious. Although no other matches were recorded that day, surely more were held. Some tournaments scheduled up to 65 matches, and visiting wrestlers taunted local athletes into taking their turn in the ring.

Dentist Doc Gibson came to Houghton from Ontario in 1900. He had played hockey, football, and lacrosse at Pickering College back home and pulled together a hockey team in the Copper Country called the Portage Lakers with himself as the star. Three years later, the seasoned Lakers claimed a world title and went on to become one of the greatest hockey teams of all times. Clarence John (Taffy) Abel from the Soo was nicknamed Mr. Hockey—although while he played for the Chicago Black Hawks, fans called him the Michigan Mountain. Abel played his first game for the Soo in 1918, and in 1924 he carried the American flag at the Olympic games held in Chamonix, France. Gibson and Abel were both inducted into the U.P. Hall of Fame in 1972.

Tauno Nurmela of Covington, inducted into the Hall of Fame in 1973, became legendary through his skills in track and field, earning 97 ribbons and medals and nine large trophy cups during his career. In some events, he bested the times of such leading athletes as Jim Thorpe and Bob Mathias. In 1924, Nurmela and some of his friends in Covington Township organized the Ponnistus Athletic Club. Always on the lookout for something interesting in the way of sports, one day the Ponnistus visited a rope-pulling tournament in Ishpeming where friends persuaded them to pull against the winning Mine 16 team. Although they had never before seen such a contest and were dressed in their Sunday best, the Ponnistus men took on Mine 16. With their spiked shoes, the men from Mine 16 all but walked over the team from Covington and then taunted the men about their loss. "In Ishpeming, we get rid of useless men like you while they are still babies," they teased.

Incensed, the Covington men went home and recruited ten of the largest, strongest men in the township. Then they set up a pole

Houghton's Barbara Arroyo (Ferries), above, competed with her brother in the Olympics. She is a member of the National Ski Hall of Fame. Cornish wrestlers, above right, wore special canvas jackets with strong collars and cuffs, and sleeves 18 to 22 inches in length.

174

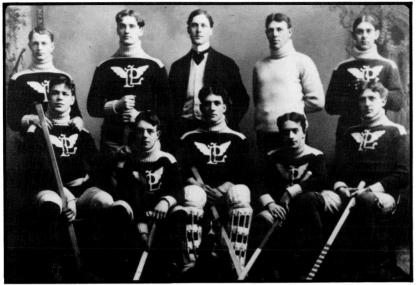

photo courtesy of Superior View, Marquette

photo courtesy of Ski Hall of Fame, Ishpeming

with a pulley at the top and a rope tied to a bucket filled with 400 pounds of rocks as a counter-balance. Pulling against the rocks, the team worked out regularly. Next they bought ten pairs of good solid shoes and had blacksmith Gust Leino make spikes twice as long as those worn by the Mine 16 team and rivet them to the soles. On the day of the next scheduled event, Covington beat Republic on the first draw, and faced Mine 16 on the second. This time, the Covington men dug in and pulled across the grass with their spikes cutting a furrow like a newly plowed field, breaking the hold of their formidable opposition. With a scowl, the Covington coach took his revenge. "In our neck of the woods," he said, "we let our men grow up, and then we decide if they're going to be men or sissies." With that, Covington took their spiked shoes and went home, never to enter rope-pulling competition again.

In the early days, ice skaters dotted the frozen lakes and ponds of the U.P. wearing colorful hand-knitted mittens, while women were dressed in long wool skirts to keep out the cold. Couples often glided across the ice in time to a waltz, particularly in Calumet where music was provided by the Calumet & Hecla Band, quartered in a nearby cupola. By the time Barbara Marchetti DeSchepper of Norway laced on her skates, the tempo had picked up. Beginning in 1950, DeSchepper won 11 major skating championships and tied for two more. Inducted into the Hall of Fame in 1976, she established three world and five American records, and was the only person to hold or share simultaneously the big four titles in speed skating: the National Indoor and Outdoor, and the North American Indoor and Outdoor Championships.

An expert at retaining his footing on a swirling log, William Girard, Sr. of Gladstone won the world championship in logrolling in 1926 and 1929, and held the old-timer's title in 1951, 1952, and 1953. Born to champion logrolling parents, Girard's specialities were trick and fancy birling. He retired in 1954 but could not resist one more try. The following year, at the age of 62, Girard participated in a logrolling exhibition in Manistique. In 1975, he was inducted into the U.P. Sports Hall of Fame.

At the turn of the century, men were playing basketball in meeting halls or dance halls with high ceilings. By 1910, girls' teams

Paul Bietila, above, was a member of the Ishpeming Ski Club when he posed for this studio portrait. He later died from a ski jumping accident. Members of the Portage Lake Hockey Team, above left, were U.S. champions in 1902-3.

had been organized. Basketball was a rough-and-tumble game, with few fouls, and almost anything was allowed short of breaking opponents' arms and legs. When a game grew too lively, chicken wire was strung across the floor to separate the few rows of spectators from the players, for the protection of both. Basketball players were dedicated to the sport. In 1927, George Butler promised that his Grand Marais players who stuck to training would get a 25-mile car trip to Seney, followed by a train ride to Marquette to participate in a basketball tournament. On the day of the tournament, the team awoke to a blinding blizzard and impassable roads. Undaunted, the boys showed up at Butler's door, ready to go. A promise was a promise, they said. "So I told them," Butler recalled later, "that if they could produce notes from their parents and the school board, we would snowshoe to Seney and catch the 6 p.m. train to Marquette."

The notes were produced, and in short order the boys strapped on snowshoes and headed for Seney. Halfway there, however, spirits began to lag. The snow had turned sticky, and it was already well into the afternoon. Butler ordered the strongest boys to the front of the line to break trail and sent a couple of the fastest boys ahead to hold the train. Five miles outside of Seney, they let out a loud shout as they spotted a truck waiting in the road to take them to the train. When they finally got to Marquette, Butler hustled the team up the hill to be checked by a physician, who gave each player a turn in the vibrator chair in an attempt to loosen stiffened muscles. Grand Marais lost the game that night, but nobody seemed to care. The team had made it to the tournament.

Clifford "Kip" Crase was a basketball star and class valedictorian in Rockland High School in 1956. Three years later, while returning with friends to his Air Force base, he was in an auto accident that left him paralyzed. He worked diligently for five years to regain total use of his limbs. When Crase recovered sufficiently to enroll at the University of Illinois as a business administration major, he was spotted by the swimming coach who suggested he try out for the sport. Crase did, and in 1965, he took fifth place in the national games in New York. Later, he also took medals in pentathlon, and a total of 65 gold, silver, and bronze medals in national

These athletes are members of the Ishpeming Hockey Team. In 1931, the skilled players won the Upper Peninsula Intermediate Championship.

photo courtesy of Marquette County Historical Society

176

and international wheelchair sports competitions. In 1968, he was awarded the breast stroke gold medal by Moshe Dayan in Israel, and in 1969 he was the USA team captain for the World Games in London and was named National Athlete of the Year.

Baseball hit the Upper Peninsula after the Civil War. Each community had its own team and for special tournaments semipro players were brought in. Legend has it that one of the longest home runs ever hit was in a game between Baraga and Hurontown. With a whack of the bat, a player sent the ball sailing across the field toward a passing freighter, where it landed on the deck. It was found later when the boat docked in Houghton, several miles away.

James Rouman of Gladstone, 1977 inductee into the Hall of Fame, was written up in Ripley's Believe It or Not in 1957 because of his 43 straight victories during five baseball seasons. Rouman was an all-around athlete and a lifelong hunter and fisherman. He also left his mark in the field of conservation at both the state and national levels, and was instrumental as executive director of the Michigan United Conservation Clubs in keeping the Porcupine Mountains as a wilderness area.

A number of outstanding athletes came from the Jesseville side of Ironwood. Edward Simonich, for example, was tops in high school shot put for several years, only to be beaten by his younger brother Rudy. After high school, Ed went to South Bend, Indiana to visit a sister and stayed to play football for Notre Dame. Folks in Indiana called Ed "the one-man gang" and declared he had been born with a football in his hand. The 1977 U.P. Sports Hall of Fame inductee coached sports for many years. When he developed cancer, he fought it as he had fought so many sports battles. "Whether it is a football game or the game of life, don't ever quit," he told his players. When he died, Ed Simonich was paid this tribute: "He kept on hand a small stock of goods, each item genuine, each one priceless—consisting of honesty, integrity, courage, intelligence, and honor. None was for sale; all were freely given. He worked at only one level—his best."

U.P. interest in football began in about 1890. In the early days, football coaches sometimes joined the lineup themselves, beefing up the backfield to help their boys win. Each team was allowed

photo courtesy of Marquette County Historical Society

Logrolling has been a popular pastime in the Upper Peninsula since early logging days. Lumberjacks got plenty of balancing practice as they drove the rivers.

177

photo courtesy of R.J. Wall, Jr.

photo courtesy of Superior View, Marquette

six downs, a touchdown scored four points, and extra points scored two. Calumet High School produced both George Gipp and Heartley (Hunk) Anderson, who were on the original list of U.P. Sports Hall of Fame inductees in 1972. Anderson started playing football when he was 12 years old. During high school he had no competition in football from George Gipp because Gipp was playing baseball. Raised as a Methodist, Gipp chose to attend Notre Dame simply because he had friends there. The tall, rangy Copper Country boy was not interested in football but he consented to try it at the request of Knute Rockne.

Gipp's high school teammates back home had said he could hit baseball drives 400 feet and, dressed in a football uniform, could run 100 yards in 10.2 seconds. High school teammate and college football rival Joe Michica said that at one practice session Gipp stood under one goal post with a strong wind at his back and kicked a football over the other goal post 100 yards away. As a Notre Dame freshman against Western State Normal, he drop-kicked a 62-yard field goal, a record which stood for several years. When he went back home to Laurium, Gipp persuaded Anderson to come to Notre Dame and join the team.

A law student, the Gipper was only mildly interested in academics, and in 1919 he was expelled from Notre Dame. Some accounts said he skipped too many classes. Another said he was caught coming out of a notorious dance hall off-limits to Notre Dame students. Gipp was eventually reinstated after the administration was deluged with demands for his return from fans.

There were those who said George Gipp paid his way through Notre Dame with his gambling—he was known to mix gambling with sports. During one game, with Notre Dame trailing Army 17-14, Coach Rockne was winding down one of his fiery half time speeches when he noticed the Gipper lounging casually against a locker. "I don't suppose you have any interest in this game?" Rockne asked.

"You're wrong there," Gipp answered. "I have $500 bet on it, and I don't intend to blow my money."

During his years at Notre Dame, Gipp brought the Fighting Irish to national prominence as one of football's top teams. In 32

Mary Agnes Wall, above, sights in a putt. The Red Jacket Fat Men's Base Ball Team, above right, posed for this photograph in 1904. Total weight of the team was 2,488 pounds. The heaviest man weighed 314 pounds.

photo courtesy of Superior View, Marquette

college games, he scored 83 touchdowns, and in the last 20 games of his career, he helped Notre Dame win 19 and tie one, to total 506 points to the opponents' 97. In Gipp's four years of college football, not one opponent pass was completed in his territory. He seemed invincible. But in the 1920 season, a shoulder injury and sore throat kept him on the sidelines for most of the Northwestern game. It was the next-to-last game. As the crowd yelled, "Gipp! Gipp! Bring on the Gipper," Gipp stepped forward, and Rockne reluctantly allowed him in for a few plays. Although he came through with a 45-yard touchdown pass which won the game, Gipp was tired. Two weeks later, he left a team banquet, complaining of a sore throat. He was put in the hospital, where for three weeks he fought a losing battle against pneumonia and streptoccia infection, kept alive with blood transfusions donated by his teammates. One evening as Rockne leaned over Gipp's bed to tell him about his selection as Notre Dame's first All-American, Gipp made his famous request. "Sometime, Rock, when the team's up against it, when things are wrong, when the breaks are beating the boys, tell them to go in with all they've got and win one for the Gipper. I don't know where I'll be then, but I'll know about it and I'll be happy." Classes were cancelled at Notre Dame when the Gipper died.

Only once did Rockne respond to Gipp's request to tell the team to "win one for the Gipper." In 1928, the Army team had Notre Dame all but stopped in its tracks, and at half time when Rockne issued the Gipp's challenge, the players wept. During the second half, a Notre Dame fullback grabbed the ball, plunged through the mighty Army line for the winning touchdown, and cried, "There's one for the Gipper!"

In 1934, villagers in Laurium gathered Lake Superior stones and built a memorial to the Gipper at the corners of Lake Linden and Tamarack Streets. They also established a living memorial, a hometown trophy which is awarded each year to the outstanding senior at Calumet High School who excells in the areas of scholarship, athletic ability, and sportsmanship.

Not all of the athletes inducted into the U.P. Sports Hall of Fame are as famous as George Gipp. But all of them enjoyed the games they played. And all of them were "winners."

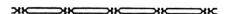

George Gipp (fourth from right) played baseball for the Calumet-Laurium team, and later gained football fame at Notre Dame under Coach Knute Rockne.

photo courtesy of Paul Pawler, Calumet

The Bangor Incident

On the afternoon of November 30, 1926, the *City of Bangor* poked her nose around Keweenaw Point and ran into one of the fiercest storms Lake Superior ever concocted. The ship carried an unusual cargo—220 brand new automobiles, mostly Chryslers, with a sprinkling of Whippets, headed toward 220 expectant owners in Duluth, Minnesota. With huge seas pounding her starboard bow and heavy snows blotting visibility, the *Bangor* got only halfway to Eagle Harbor before she was forced to come about and retrace her course to Keweenaw Point, aiming for the protected waters of Bete Grise. She never made it. The steam-powered steering gear broke, and despite the efforts of the two seamen wrestling the stern wheel, the ship wallowed fearfully in 25-foot troughs. At 6:00 p.m. she ran hard onto a reef just two miles west of Keweenaw Point, and there the *City of Bangor* finished out her life.

Fortunately, the reef was but a short distance from shore, and in the lee of the ship, the men had little difficulty getting their lifeboats launched and across the narrow gap to safety. The solid land was comforting to legs which had been arguing for stability, but it was the only comfort those legs were to enjoy during the 48 hours that followed.

The first night was spent in the vicinity of the ship. Concern for medical supplies and food, which were encased in a sheath of ice, was lost in the joy of salvation, the warmth of roaring fires, and the expectations of a morning rescue. But morning brought only more snow, and the combined gnawing of hunger and uneasiness quickly replaced optimism. By afternoon, it was obvious that help was nowhere in sight, and at 3:30 p.m., the crew headed out to find it.

Under good conditions, the men could have negotiated the six miles to Copper Harbor in time for a late supper, but knee-deep snow, zero temperatures, and low-cut shipboard footwear made it a perilous journey. To compound their problems, during a brief lull in the storm, the men caught a glimpse of the East Bluff behind them which they mistook for Brockway Mountain, a familiar landmark of previous voyages. Believing they had somehow missed Copper Harbor, they retraced their steps several miles before discovering the error. It took great effort and courage to keep numb legs moving into a wind that turned their labored breath into frost and threatened to drive it back whence it came. But the combined urging of the ship's five officers got the 24-man crew through the long afternoon and even longer night. It was mid-afternoon of the

The ill-fated cargo of the City of Bangor *spent the winter lined up in front of Charley Maki's house in Copper Harbor. As soon as the roads could be plowed, local drivers were paid $5 each to motor the vehicles caravan-style back to Detroit for reconditioning.*

photo courtesy of Michigan Technological University Archives and Copper Country Historical Collection

photo from the Tony Uranesich Collection

next day, and 10,000 stumbles later, before help arrived.

Captain Tony Glaza and his Coast Guard crew from Eagle Harbor were returning to their station with the crew of the steamer *Maythem,* herself aground near Point Isabelle, when he sighted the *Bangor's* crew wallowing through the snow near Horseshoe Harbor. Captain Glaza raced for Copper Harbor, deposited his passengers at Fred the Swede's saloon and hostel, then quickly returned to pick up the crew from the *City of Bangor.* Some of the men had frosted feet and all were sorely drained by their struggle through snowdrifts, brush, and swamps. They were also mighty hungry, as it had been 48 hours since they had last eaten. Fred the Swede didn't have nearly enough food for such a crew, so other accommodations had to be found.

Billy Bergh and his thirteen-year-old son, Howard, were returning from chores in the barn when the faint figure of an oilskin-clad human approaching from the east was seen through the snow-muffled night. The occupant of the oilskins was a Coast Guardsman leading the *Bangor's* crew on a search for lodging and food. They found both at Billy Bergh's house.

Top right is the City of Bangor, *driven hard onto a reef two miles west of Keweenaw Point. Her cargo of Chryslers and Whippets, bottom right, was later chopped free of the icy deck and winched from the hold.*

182

While Mrs. Bergh and her daughter, Helga, made preparations for their 29 unexpected guests, Howard and his younger brother lit kerosene lamps and set out to guide the men of the *Bangor* to their house. It was only a few hundred yards' walk, but during the brief pause at the Swede's, exhausted muscles had stiffened and drowsiness had taken hold. Unaware of the condition of the crew, young Howard couldn't understand why grown men would stumble and fall so often.

It was not just by chance that the Bergh's hospitality was sought, for it was common knowledge that their two pigs had been recently butchered, and that they maintained the only reliable cows in Copper Harbor. Perhaps Mrs. Bergh worried some as she noticed her winter's larder dwindle, yet her only apparent concern was for the hungry men. Captain Glaza's boat returned to Copper Harbor several days later to pick up the *Bangor* crew, but a strong northeaster kept him at Bergh's dock long enough for harbor ice to seal things in for the winter. Charley Maki's sleigh and similar vehicles transported the men to Calumet, and as soon as they were able to travel, they returned by rail to their homes.

During the *Bangor's* wild voyage, the seas whipped 18 automobiles from the deck, and they still reside somewhere between—and slightly below—Horseshoe and Copper Harbors. The remaining vehicles on deck when the ship grounded were soon encased in ice. In mid-December, during a quiet stretch of weather, the vehicles were chopped free, and winched from the hold, then lowered by ramp to the ice. Teams cleared a road along the ice to Copper Harbor, and soon after Christmas the vehicles were driven to the Harbor under their own power and lined up in front of Charley Maki's house for the winter.

Next year's Chryslers were already on the drawing board, so it was imperative that the *City of Bangor* vehicles be returned to Detroit for reconditioning and put back on the market as soon as possible—that being whenever the road between Copper Harbor and Phoenix could be opened. No attempt was made before March, and even then, it was a two-week chore for Houghton and Keweenaw County plows, assisted by a unit from Albert Lea, Minnesota. It marked the first time that stretch of U.S. 41 was plowed.

William Nicholson of Calumet, one owner of the *Bangor,* visited the wreck the following summer and decided she was a total loss. The ship was sold to the T.L. Durocher Company of Detour but salvage operations did not get under way until the spring of 1928. In the meantime, the *Bangor* had been joined by the steamer *Altadoc,* also driven ashore during a storm, and the two ships shared the solitude of another winter on Keweenaw Point. Durocher never finished cutting up the *Bangor* for scrap, and in the 1940s it was resold to the Kenneth Straight Salvage Engineers who completed the salvage.

Today, no physical traces of the *Bangor* remain on the Keweenaw landscape unless, of course, you were to look through the window of Paddy Slusarzyk's garage in Calumet. She's not as shiny as she used to be, and it's been several years since she's been out on the open road. But her engine still turns over upon request, and that's about all you can ask of a 1926 Chrysler which arrived in Keweenaw aboard the *City of Bangor.*

Authors

William Barkell and **Wilbert (Wimpy) E. Salmi,** both of Hancock, combined their skills to produce *STRIKE!* Barkell is president of the Houghton County Historical Society and Salmi is the organization's vice president. **Ted Bays** of Marquette is a wood cutter and a freelance writer of Upper Peninsula based fiction and local history. Escanaba native **Frank Bourke** has long had an interest in rail-

Barkell   Salmi   Bays   Bourke   Boyum   Carter

Cooper   DeLongchamp   Deo   Dunham   Franklin   Frimodig

roads and history, and he has authored a number of writings on both. **Burton H. Boyum** of Ishpeming went to work for the Cleveland-Cliffs Iron Company in 1941, and is now retained by the company as a consultant. **Jim Carter** was raised in Grand Marais and currently lives in Marquette. He is director of Northern Michigan University's news bureau and the University Press. **James Cooper** was working at Porcupine Mountain State Park when he wrote *The Great Ontonagon Fire.* He now trains and shows horses in Colorado. Born and reared in the Ishpeming area, **Shirley DeLongchamp** is a freelance writer of history and U.P. travel. **Jack Deo** specializes in handling old photographs at his Superior View studio in Marquette. He provided and hand tinted many of the historic photos that appear in this book. **Tom Dunham** was director of the Bayliss Public Library in Sault Ste. Marie when he wrote *Taming the St. Mary's.* He now lives in Lancaster, Ohio. **Dixie Franklin** of Marquette is an award winning freelance writer published in several magazines and newspapers throughout the Midwest. **David M. (Mac) Frimodig** of Laurium had a 30-year career with Michigan's Department of Natural Resources. At the time of his retirement in 1978, he was information officer for the Upper Peninsula. **David T. Halkola** of Hancock is a professor of history at Michigan Technological University, and previously served for five years as president of Suomi College. As Cultural Resources Specialist for Isle Royale National Park, **Carol Maass** spends six months living in Beacon Hill and the other six on Isle Royale. St. Ignace resident **Wesley H. Maurer, Jr.** is publisher-editor of the *St. Ignace News,* and associate publisher of the *Mackinac Island Town Crier.* Born in Ironwood,

Halkola   Maass   Maurer   Maurin   Oikarinen   Pilon

Pyle   Rood   Rydholm   Segall   Vander Hill   Wright

Ray Maurin is a freelance writer and photographer, active in all phases of community theater, and curator of the Ironwood Historical Museum. Copper Country native **Peter Oikarinen** lives in Calumet and has written a number of books about people in the Upper Peninsula, and also a book of poems and short stories. Sugar Island resident **Roger Pilon** works for the Eastern Upper Peninsula Regional Planning and Development Commission, and is a stalker of local history. East Lansing resident **Susan Newhof Pyle** is a writer of natural history and travel, and has worked for *Michigan Natural Resources Magazine* as editorial assistant. **Dave Rood** of Gladstone has an enviable background in the newspaper business and presently writes a widely circulated award winning weekly column. **Fred Rydholm** of Lakewood is a retired school teacher with a life-long interest in local history, and he has a book on the history of Marquette County in progress. Lansing resident **Glenna Segall** is marketing manager for *Michigan Natural Resources Magazine.* **Warren Vander Hill** is director of the Honors College at Ball State University in Muncie, Indiana, and is working on a history of the immigrant groups in the Midwest. **Leianne F. Wright** is an illustrator and designer based in Lansing, and is a graphics assistant for *Michigan Natural Resources Magazine.*

Acknowledgements

We are grateful to many individuals and organizations who assisted in preparing A Most Superior Land. *Their contributions of time, talent, and enthusiasm—not to mention patience—have helped make this book a worthy tribute to all the men and women who have called the Upper Peninsula "home." We offer sincere thanks to the following:*

To members of the historical societies of Marquette, Alger, Chippewa, and Delta Counties for opening their files and letting us make use of their vast information resources; to Judy Dow, Richard Hathaway, and Richard Lucas of the Library of Michigan at Lansing for their many hours spent locating maps and out-of-print books and magazines needed for this project, and for allowing us to make generous use of them; to Kitti Frimodig for organizing the General Foreman; to Earl Jacobson and Michael Anuta for assisting David Halkola in the preparation of Ivory Towers; *to Betsy Youngblood for initial manuscript editing; to Vicki Booth, Ruth Jones, Kathy Tran, and Laurie Tran for typesetting and production work; to John Felsing, Jr. for assisting with the book's graphics; to Leroy Barnett of the Michigan State Archives for assistance in locating elusive train maps late on a Friday afternoon; to John Curry for his scrupulous maintenance of the Michigan State Archives' magnificent collection of photographs, and for assisting us with eleventh-hour photo needs; to Lake Superior State College for invaluable information regarding the questing of unicorns including hunting season dates, bag limits, legal lures, and for assorted proprieties associated with the event; to Jim Purvis for giving new meaning to the word "proofreading"; to Gijsbert van Frankenhuyzen for adding his graphics excellence to this project; to photographer David Kenyon for skillfully producing a myriad of "rush" orders with never a whimper, and for enthusiastically joining in our constant search for "just one more photo..."; to Richard Morscheck for editorial and production support, and for knowing when to put out small fires and when to set them; to Russell McKee whose dreams gave this book its beginnings, and whose determination gave it breath; and finally, to the husbands, wives, and lovers who endured late suppers, work-filled weekends, and the preoccupied ramblings of the writers, editors, and artists who produced* A Most Superior Land. ◄▲

Susan Newhof Pyle
Editor

photo courtesy of Superior View, Marquette

Index